ISSUE 18, JULY 2023

AUSTRALIAN FOREIGN AFFAIRS

The Fix

Reviews

Correspondence

Contributors

Andrew Carr is a senior lecturer in the Strategic and Defence Studies Centre at the Australian National University.

Erin Cook is a writer and analyst based in South-East Asia. She produces the Dari Mulut ke Mulut newsletter.

Dennis Glover is a political speechwriter, journalist and novelist, and a graduate of Monash and Cambridge universities.

Michael J. Green is a professor and CEO at the US Studies Centre at the University of Sydney.

Mei-fen Kuo is a lecturer of contemporary Chinese culture and history at Macquarie University.

Mary-Louise O'Callaghan is a journalist and writer who lives in Solomon Islands and was RAMSI's public affairs manager from 2006 to 2013.

Sam Roggeveen is director of the Lowy Institute's International Security Program and author of the forthcoming *The Echidna Strategy: Australia's Search for Power and Peace.*

Emma Shortis is a historian, writer and commentator focused on the history and politics of the United States.

Australian Foreign Affairs is published three times a year by Australian Foreign Affairs Pty Ltd. Publisher: Morry Schwartz. CEO: Rebecca Costello. Editor-in-chief: Erik Jensen. ISBN 978-1-76064-4253 ISSN 2208-5912 Subscriptions – 1 year print & digital auto-renew (3 issues): $49.99 within Australia incl. GST. 1 year print and digital subscription (3 issues): $59.99 within Australia incl. GST. 2 year print & digital (6 issues): $114.99 within Australia incl. GST. 1 year digital only auto-renew: $29.99. Payment may be made by MasterCard, Visa or Amex, or by cheque made out to Schwartz Books Pty Ltd. Payment includes postage and handling. To subscribe, fill out the form inside this issue, subscribe online at www.australianforeignaffairs.com, email subscribe@australianforeignaffairs.com or phone 1800 077 514 / 61 3 9486 0288. Correspondence should be addressed to: The Editor, Australian Foreign Affairs, 22–24 Northumberland Street, Collingwood, VIC, 3066 Australia Phone: 61 3 9486 0288 / Fax: 61 3 9486 0244 Email: enquiries@australianforeignaffairs.com. Editor: Jonathan Pearlman. Deputy Editor: Kate Morgan. Associate Editor: Chris Feik. Consulting Editor: Allan Gyngell. Publicity: Anna Lensky. Design: Peter Long. Production Coordination: Marilyn de Castro. Typesetting: Tristan Main. Cover photograph: AP Photo/Evan Vucci. Printed in Australia by McPherson's Printing Group.

Editor's Note

WE NEED TO TALK ABOUT AMERICA

For decades, the United States was not only the most important feature of Australia's defence and foreign policy outlook, it was also arguably the least interesting.

Defence white papers, for instance, have tended to present the US alliance as the bedrock of Australia's security, but the real areas of concern in these documents were the intentions and capabilities of our potential rivals and neighbours, not of our closest friend. America's dominance, and staying power, were taken for granted.

But all that has changed.

The United States is no longer the unrivalled power in Asia. China is the world's largest trading nation, and is, by some measures, the largest economy. It is undertaking a massive military build-up, and, according to modelling by defence analysts, could either defeat the United States in a war over Taiwan or inflict such heavy costs that the global status of both powers would be undermined. In 2009, Australia's Defence White Paper stated: "No other power will have the military, economic or strategic capacity to challenge US global primacy over the period covered by this White Paper [to 2030]." In 2023, the Defence Strategic Review stated: "No longer is our Alliance partner, the United States, the unipolar leader of the Indo-Pacific."

Even during the heady years after the end of the Cold War, Canberra's outlook included the warning that Washington's unrivalled status may one day be tested; its commitment to the region could no longer be presumed. That day has now arrived.

But the other reason to reassess the role and trajectory of the United States has involved developments within its borders. In 2016, the American people elected a president who threatened to upend alliances, lauded authoritarians, imposed tariffs on friends and then refused to accept an election result. He is running again in 2024. Anthony Albanese has insisted that deals such as AUKUS – Australia's security pact with the United States and the United Kingdom – are agreements between nations and are not dependent on leaders. But he has also insisted that the United States–Australia relationship rests on shared values, a claim that suggests that ties might fray if those values decouple.

Whether we like it or not, the trajectory, reliability and capability of the United States are now questions rather than axioms. Australia needs to start understanding these changes and their consequences, and considering potential responses.

A tribute to Allan Gyngell

It is no overstatement to say that the death of Allan Gyngell in May represented a genuine loss to Australia and left the country without a figure who, with warmth and good humour, enhanced its capacity to navigate its challenges in the international arena.

Allan's career was distinguished: he served as a diplomat, was an adviser to Prime Minister Paul Keating, headed the Lowy Institute, the Office of National Assessments and the Australian Institute for International Affairs, and wrote *Fear of Abandonment* (published by La Trobe University Press, a joint imprint with Black Inc.). He was also consulting editor of Australian Foreign Affairs, which allowed me to experience – as so many others in Australia have – his unfailing generosity, wisdom and thoughtfulness.

In his many public roles, and from his reading and conversations, he amassed a deep reservoir of knowledge about Australia and its region – and, armed with his generosity and his commitment to public life, he became an unparalleled source of guidance to policymakers, diplomats, academics, analysts and journalists.

His approach to foreign policy reflected his personal temperament: he was calm, curious, kind and fair, willing to be persuaded and willing to stand his ground. In an era in which politics is deeply partisan, Allan's counsel was sought and trusted by those on all sides of the divides – from hawks and doves, and from politicians of all stripes. He was not guided by ego or ideology; if anything, his single guiding dogma was that nothing, really, is unprecedented – that history and experience are the best tools for understanding the world and how to respond to its challenges.

Penny Wong, Australia's foreign minister, described him as "our finest mind in Australian foreign policy". He will be greatly missed.

Jonathan Pearlman

TARGET AUSTRALIA

Is the alliance making us less safe?

Sam Roggeveen

Last October, the ABC's investigative journalism program *Four Corners* revealed news that sent ripples through Australia's national debate about defence policy, but ought to have made waves. The revelation, subsequently confirmed by government, was that Australia and the United States had agreed to expand the RAAF Tindal air base, around 300 kilometres south of Darwin, so that up to six American strategic bombers could operate from there.

Australia has supported US bomber rotations in the Northern Territory since at least 2006, but, with this air base refurbishment, the US and Australia are effectively integrating RAAF Tindal into America's war planning. Australia had previously hosted US bombers for training purposes, but this initiative will allow American bombers to fly operational missions from Australian soil, including in wartime.

If the Tindal decision passed with little comment, the same cannot be said of the 14 March AUKUS announcement in San Diego, California: Australia would acquire three to five second-hand Virginia-class nuclear-powered attack submarines (SSNs) from the US, and then a class of new-generation submarines designed and built with help from the US and the UK, to be known as SSN AUKUS. Prime ministers Albanese and Sunak, alongside President Biden, also announced Submarine Rotational Force-West: from as early as 2027, the UK will rotate one SSN through the newly refurbished HMAS Stirling naval base in Western Australia, while the US would contribute four. Australia has also committed to developing a new A$10 billion east coast base for its nuclear-powered submarines. It too will be capable of supporting US and UK submarines.

Almost all observers agree that these initiatives signal a closer Australian alignment with American foreign policy objectives – they will bring Australia into a tighter American embrace and increase the likelihood that Australia will fight alongside the US should Washington and Beijing go to war, whether over Taiwan or for another reason. The Carnegie Endowment's Ashley Townshend rightly described it as a "transformation in the character and purpose of the US–Australia alliance: one that will see Australia play an increasingly pivotal role in actively supporting US military operations as part of a strategy of collective deterrence." The real point of dispute is whether this closer alignment serves Australia's interests. The answer to that question rests partly on the costs Australia is likely to bear, and one of those costs will be an increased likelihood of Chinese military assault on Australia.

Bombers

Six bombers may sound like a modest fleet for RAAF Tindal to accommodate, but the US bomber fleet only numbers around 140, made up of the B-52H Stratofortress, B-1B Lancer and B-2 stealth bombers. Each of these aircraft can generate significant combat power: a single B-52H can carry twenty cruise missiles, or 120 missiles for a six-aircraft strike package. Cruise missiles are capable and expensive, so in a war with China they would likely be used for high-value fixed targets such as command centres, airfields, bridges, communications centres and power stations. The missions performed by these bombers could have a nuclear dimension too. Media coverage in the wake of the *Four Corners* scoop placed a lot of emphasis on America's bombers being "nuclear capable", but that is something of a distraction. US bombers don't routinely carry nuclear weapons, and certainly not to airfields that aren't specifically designed to accommodate them. America's air-launched nuclear weapons are only stored in five countries outside America, all in Europe, at bases built to higher-than-normal security standards. If the United States ever wanted to store nuclear weapons at RAAF Tindal, such a move would be preceded by long political debate in Australia, and we would observe specific building works and security upgrades at the base. That is not the intention right now.

Yet even without nuclear weapons, US bombers flying out of Tindal could play an important role in the nuclear balance between America and China because they could be tasked with striking China's nuclear infrastructure, such as missile silos and bases, command and control facilities, early warning radars that let China know of an impending nuclear attack, and air defence facilities designed to keep its nuclear bases safe.

It is hard to overstate the sensitivity involved in threatening another nation's nuclear forces. Every nuclear-armed nation goes to enormous expense to make their arsenals inviolable so that they always have a last-ditch defence, a guaranteed capability to cause unacceptable damage to an adversary even if every other defence has failed. If China was losing a war against the United States, its nuclear arsenal would ensure that such a loss could be contained. China's territory and political system would not be under threat because as a last resort, it could threaten the US with nuclear strikes. But China's nuclear arsenal is not inviolable. It numbers around 400 operational warheads compared to 1700 for the US, and its delivery systems are not all world-class. China's nuclear force is growing rapidly but remains vulnerable to a surprise attack that would leave it defenceless.

Australia wants the capability to strike targets on Chinese soil

In sum, Tindal could not only help the US win a conventional (non-nuclear) war, but also play a part in neutralising China's nuclear forces. It is clear why American bombers flying out of RAAF Tindal would be an important target for Chinese forces.

Submarine bases

Submarine Rotational Force-West and the new east coast submarine base are also likely to present important new targets for China because they, too, will directly support US military operations. The submarines operating from there might be tasked with protecting an aircraft carrier battle group from enemy ships and submarines. They could also operate independently to find and destroy Chinese warships supporting an invasion of Taiwan, or possibly cargo vessels if the US was trying to enforce a blockade of Chinese ports. American and British attack submarines are also capable of striking land targets thousands of kilometres inland with their onboard Tomahawk cruise missiles. As with the bombers from RAAF Tindal, the range and precision of these missiles means they would likely be assigned to high-value targets.

And, like the Tindal-based bombers, there would be a nuclear dimension to US submarine operations conducted from Australian ports. China's nuclear arsenal has previously been heavily weighted towards land-based weapons – that is, missiles fired from silos or mobile launchers on Chinese territory. To improve the survivability of its nuclear deterrent, China has in recent years put more of its nuclear arsenal onboard missile-firing submarines, known as SSBNs. The US and Soviet Union have been doing this since the late 1950s, but China, despite its otherwise rapid military modernisation, remains a laggard in submarine technology. From 2007 it began rolling out the Type 094 SSBN, but the slow commissioning pace for this type indicates that China's technological problems continue. It is believed the Type 096 will eventually replace this class and become China's first truly modern SSBN, but this is still years away. In the meantime, China has put a portion of its nuclear arsenal onboard noisy submarines whose missiles cannot reach the US from home waters. In wartime, the job of American submarines, some of which will operate from Australian bases, will be to hunt and destroy these SSBNs. Should they succeed, China would only have its land-based missiles left to deter the United States, and those, too, might be vulnerable to pre-emptive strikes.

Australian submarines and missiles

In February 2023, Prime Minister Albanese boasted that nuclear-powered submarines represent "the single biggest leap in our defence capability in our history". He's right. Assuming the submarines are delivered, they will represent a major boost in Australia's military capabilities because nuclear-powered submarines are so much more effective than the diesel-powered boats we now operate. Nuclear power allows submarines to operate at higher sustained speeds, with infinite range and endurance. The only limits are crew stamina and food supplies. Nuclear boats are also larger, which means they can carry more weapons.

Australia could use its nuclear-powered submarine fleet to defend the continent from military aggression close to our shores. Australia has a huge coastline, after all, so submarines with long endurance and high speed would be useful. But while the government is reluctant to say exactly what it wants the new submarine fleet to do, it seems clear that the intent is not to protect Australia's coastline directly but to operate thousands of kilometres to our north. Defence Minister Richard Marles says he wants the ADF to "hold potential adversaries' forces at risk at a distance". When AUKUS was announced, then Australian ambassador to the US Arthur Sinodinos said, "We want to be able to ... project our power further up, rather than taking an approach that all our defence has to be a defence of the mainland." Nuclear-powered submarines would be ideally suited to operating off the coast of China, hemming the PLA Navy in home waters. And the requirement for the new submarines to carry Tomahawk cruise missiles can only be interpreted one way: Australia wants the capability to strike targets on Chinese soil.

Simply having such a fleet will raise expectations in Washington that we would use it to help the United States in a war against China. By the mid-2030s Australia is expected to have three Virginia-class SSNs in service. To have one SSN ready for war at any time, a navy needs three at a minimum, so this is the point at which Australia could begin to contribute to a conflict. By then, Australia will have spent more than a decade in the most intimate of partnerships with the US, stretching across engineering, nuclear safety and security, weapons and combat systems, as well as tactics and operating procedures. The whole purpose of this enterprise will be to improve Australian and American capacity to jointly deter – and, if necessary, to fight – China. Having made that kind of investment, it seems unlikely that Australia would withhold it at the critical moment.

How important would these submarines be to a US-led military effort against China? When former prime minister Paul Keating said Australia's proposed fleet of eight submarines was akin to "throwing toothpicks at the mountain", he underestimated the ambition of the project and the potency it promises to deliver. Even the UK and France don't boast attack submarine fleets of this size. China has only six nuclear-powered attack submarines, though that number will grow in coming decades. The US Navy estimates it will have sixty-six nuclear-powered attack submarines in service by 2050. If we assume all eight of Australia's boats are in service by that time, Australia would be adding roughly 12 per cent to the US fleet. Australia's fleet will significantly enhance any US-led fight against China, and thus they will be important targets.

Because of their greater speed, endurance and weapons capabilities, these SSNs will certainly be more of a threat to China than the twelve French-designed submarines Australia had earlier planned to acquire. An American Center for Strategic and Budgetary Assessments study from 2013 concluded that, operating from Western Australia, it would take three times as long for a diesel submarine to reach China's southern waters as it would a nuclear-powered boat, and once there the diesel boat could stay on station for eleven days versus seventy-seven days for the nuclear submarine.

In the event of war, what would the AUKUS submarines do when operating near Chinese waters? Their missions would likely be similar to the US SSN missions described earlier: sinking Chinese naval ships and submarines, blockading ports or striking targets on the Chinese landmass with long-range cruise missiles. One difference, however, is that, owing to the sensitivity of nuclear weapons arsenals, particularly during a war that could easily go nuclear, the United States would be unlikely to subordinate nuclear-related missions to Australia's submarine fleet, such as striking China's nuclear infrastructure on land or sinking China's small fleet of ballistic-missile submarines. Still, owing to their range and endurance, Australian SSNs will be more likely to encounter a Chinese ballistic-missile submarines in the course of their operations. It will be a thorny doctrinal question for Australia whether, even during full-scale hostilities, an Australian SSN would try to destroy such a target or leave it be. SSBNs are critical to any nuclear-armed nation's assurance that its arsenal is secure. If even one was sunk, it could trigger a disastrous escalation.

The AUKUS agreement also includes cooperative research on hypersonic weapons, which Australia aims to field in years to come. The mission for these weapons is not yet clear, but if they are eventually acquired for the purpose of hitting targets on the Chinese mainland from bases or mobile platforms on Australian soil, the risks of Chinese strikes on Australia are raised still higher, because there is no effective defence against such weapons.

Clearly, having these capabilities raises the likelihood of Chinese military strikes against Australia. But we can go further: they make it more likely that a crisis will escalate into a war, because they incentivise China to launch a pre-emptive surprise attack. In a crisis with the

United States which is poised on the brink of conflict, China may feel it is in its interests to strike before Australia's submarines leave port and before its hypersonic missiles are dispersed to remote locations, simply because it is so much easier to target fixed sites. In turn, this creates an incentive for Australia to pre-empt the pre-emptor. We would be tempted to use our weapons before we lose them.

It is important not to overstate this point. If a war broke out right now, there would be little reason for China to strike Australian targets because the Australian Defence Force presents a small threat (the US–Australia joint facilities at Pine Gap and North West Cape are possible exceptions, but because those facilities play an important role in US nuclear deterrence, China might exempt them in order to signal that it does not intend to escalate a conflict to nuclear use). But, in a future crisis, Australia's new force – SSNs and hypersonic missiles, plus American bomber and SSN facilities on Australian soil – will raise its profile in the eyes of Chinese military planners. When these facilities and capabilities come online, China's military calculation will be different, and so will the psychology of deterrence between the two countries. Crisis stability will have eroded.

Australia will be a bigger target

The political symbolism of Australian strikes against Chinese territory also increases the danger to Australian territory because China would be unlikely to let such a blow by a much smaller power pass without retaliation. Advocates of Australian long-range strike argue that the ability to hit adversaries is critical to deterrence. As former defence minister Kim Beazley put it: "I just figure you have really got to hurt people, if you're going to get a point across and they won't take much notice of you unless they know how much hurt you can inflict. That's why the F-111s were fantastic." But the F-111 was never designed to strike the Soviet Union. It was ordered by the Menzies government because it had the range to hit Jakarta. If that was indeed a "fantastic" capability, it was because Indonesia had very few means to strike us back. But in China, Australia would be facing an adversary that could inflict much more punishment on us than we could on it.

The AUKUS calculation

If a war between the United States and China erupted tomorrow and Australia decided to contribute militarily to the US side, it would not be a critical player. We could offer a destroyer and frigate to protect a US aircraft carrier from attacks by submarines, ships and aircraft. The Collins-class submarine fleet could play a role. Aerial refuelling aircraft would be in high demand, and the RAAF could offer up to seven of those. We could hunt Chinese submarines with our P-8 Poseidon maritime patrol aircraft. Perhaps the most potent capability we could offer would be to send a squadron of F-35 fighters to Japan to hit targets in China. But even if Australia did *all* of these things, given the scale of such a war, they would be niche contributions. By contrast, the combined effect of hosting US bombers and submarines, and having our own nuclear-powered submarines with the ability to hit the Chinese mainland, will substantially raise Australia's status. Australia will be a bigger target.

We should consider one further risk to Australia from the expansion of our air and naval bases to accommodate US operations, and that is the possibility of them becoming nuclear targets. In their current guise, these bases are unlikely to be important enough to get the attention of China's nuclear targeters. But as China's arsenal grows, so will its target list. And if China was losing a war against the US, it might choose to demonstrate resolve by escalating to the use of nuclear weapons. Yet because striking the US itself may induce America to retaliate rather than back down, China might instead demonstrate its firepower and political will by detonating a nuclear weapon against a US ally. In that event, the Australian bases that support US air and naval operations against China would be a fitting target.

These risks might all be worth taking, and indeed Australia has taken similar risks before. The US–Australian joint facilities at Pine Gap and North West Cape were almost certainly on Soviet nuclear targeting lists during the Cold War, and might be on China's list, too, though for now it has far fewer warheads to spare. It is also important to stress that the risk to Australia remains manageable for now because, despite the modernisation of the PLA over the last thirty years, China's military is still not very good at projecting power over the long distances required to hit Australia. That's partly because its focus has been on modernising the forces that will fight closer to home.

But also, projecting military power over thousands of kilometres is difficult and costly, especially in the absence of foreign bases.

Nevertheless, China does have land-based ballistic missiles that can reach northern Australia. It has some destroyers that could enter our northern waters and fire cruise missiles against land targets. It also has a nascent aircraft carrier fleet which could sail towards Australia, though for the moment without any evident capacity to hit land targets. It has a large bomber fleet but few aerial refuelling aircraft that would give them the range to hit anything beyond Australia's far north. All of this will change. China is developing a new generation of long-range stealth bombers, a new class of cruise-missile-firing submarines and better aircraft carriers. If anything, Australia's plans will give China an additional incentive to pursue those capabilities.

Australia takes these risks because we have concluded that, on balance, we are likely to be safer within the alliance, with all the obligations it imposes, than outside it. But if China's capabilities to strike Australia are set to increase, and if we are raising China's incentives to do so, then the judgements we have previously made about whether the risks of the alliance outweigh the security benefits need to be re-evaluated. Does the trade-off between the risk of being targeted and the security provided by the alliance still favour Australia?

The answer to that question depends on the value Australia places on US military dominance in Asia, including America's ability to decisively defeat China in a war over Taiwan. If American victory in such a war is a vital interest for Australia, then it is proper for Australia to contribute to sustaining that dominance. In February *The Sydney Morning Herald* published a three-part series called "Red Alert", in which five Australian analysts brought together to assess the Chinese military threat concluded that, should Taiwan fall to the communists in Beijing, America's position in Asia would be hopelessly compromised, China would command the entire region (this was reminiscent of Cold War fears that South-East Asia's "dominoes" would fall if South Vietnam succumbed to the communist north), and Australia would suffer under Chinese dominance:

> Japan would be in direct threat, the US military at risk of direct attack at its bases in the region. South-East Asia and the Pacific island states could then be dominated by Beijing. Australia's commercial and security lifelines to the world would operate only at Beijing's pleasure. Australia would be highly vulnerable to economic coercion, military intrusion or both. Its sovereignty would be conditional on Xi's policies towards a subject power.

"Red Alert" was wildly alarmist, but there is a strangely complacent element to this analysis too. Japanese and American bases in Asia are at high risk from China *right now*. Conquering Taiwan won't materially change that reality, given the missile forces and air bases China already has arrayed along its coast. Yet the "Red Alert" series also overstated the consequences for Australia of a Chinese victory over Taiwan. Merely possessing Taiwan won't cut off Australia's trade links with the world. The distances involved are vast (around 7400 kilometres from Taipei to Melbourne), and the size of the Australian continent imposes huge constraints on any force trying to block Australia's ports. Maintaining a blockade would be resource-intensive for China, with unclear benefits. Nor will Chinese control over Taiwan substantially increase Australia's vulnerability to Chinese military intrusion because Australia is still so far away. Australia's priority should be to ensure that China never establishes bases in the Pacific islands region rather than in faraway Taiwan. And Australia should also consider the possibility that the United States itself is less committed to Taiwan's security than is commonly believed, and indeed that its commitment to maintaining its military leadership throughout the region is waning.

Reinforcement or retrenchment?

Despite the promise of the Obama pivot and countless speeches and policy documents that put China at the centre of US security policy, the weight of military power America dedicates to the Asian theatre has not radically increased since the Soviet Union collapsed, even as China became a true military superpower over that period. The RAAF Tindal and HMAS Stirling announcements have been widely interpreted as a signal that this might finally be changing, but it is not clear that this is the case. A broad shift in US regional strategy is underway, that much is true. But what's really changing is not US force structure – the type and weight of forces committed to the region – but force *posture* – that is, where its forces are arrayed around Asia.

A strong motivation for this change is the growing threat from China's ballistic and cruise missile forces, which make many existing US bases more vulnerable. As well as RAAF Tindal and HMAS Stirling, this shift in force posture includes expanded facilities in the Larrakeyah precinct in Darwin, and a new agreement with the Philippines allowing the US to use four additional bases there. In 2022, the United States announced it was removing two fighter squadrons permanently based in Kadena, Japan, and replacing them with temporary detachments precisely because Kadena is so vulnerable to Chinese missiles. The airfield on the tiny US-controlled Pacific territory of Tinian is also being upgraded in case the larger Guam base nearby is knocked out.

These efforts will make US forces more survivable in the event of war, but it won't increase US combat power. In fact, these dispersal efforts represent a retrenchment, of sorts. For instance, America's bomber presence in Asia is presently concentrated on the island of Guam, now well within the range of China's DF-26 ballistic missile (dubbed the "Guam killer"). Tindal is outside the range of the DF-26. But moving these bombers further away from China comes with a price – it means the US can fly fewer missions, and that each mission is more costly in terms of time, fuel, maintenance, aerial tanker support and crew fatigue. In short, six bombers based in Tindal are a less potent military asset than the same number based in Guam, which means America's deterrent against China is diminishing while the military threat to Australia increases.

Submarine Rotational Force-West at HMAS Stirling may fall into the same category, although we don't yet know if this facility will be used to increase America's overall submarine presence in the region, or whether the boats rotating through there will come from its existing fleets in Honolulu and Guam. Given that Guam is within range of China's DF-26 ballistic missile, it would make sense for the US Navy to use HMAS Stirling and the future east coast base as alternative facilities. But this would repeat the problem of the US bombers at RAAF Tindal: SSNs operating from Australia's west and east coasts will be less potent than the same number operating from Guam, because they will have longer transit times.

So, the details about where these additional US SSNs will originate from are crucial. Should the US Navy commit four SSNs to this rotation which were previously committed to the continental US or other military theatres, this would represent a substantial upgrade of its overall Pacific presence. The other extreme is that the US will assign four boats from existing Pacific forces, with just one or two rotating through HMAS Stirling at any one time. The UK commitment to Submarine Rotational Force-West is also unclear, but we already know that any military capability the UK contributes will be far from decisive, and probably no more than tokenistic. Given that the UK only operates seven SSNs in total, rotations are likely to be infrequent, particularly since the Royal Navy is now quite rightly preoccupied with the threat from Russia. An occasional UK submarine visit to HMAS Stirling will not play a substantial role in balancing Chinese military power. Britain simply does not have the capability to take on such a task on the opposite side of the world when a European great power is menacing its own neighbourhood.

There is one final element of the AUKUS submarine project which raises questions about whether the US is increasing its military commitment to Australia and the region, and that regards the arrangements for the sale of three to five second-hand Virginia-class SSNs to Australia. It is unclear if the US Navy intends to replace these boats. Australia has committed to investing in US shipyards, but this money won't be used to accelerate production of new hulls to backfill the US Navy fleet following the transfer of SSNs to Australia. Rather, it will be used to improve maintenance of the remaining fleet. That should increase the availability of existing hulls, which in operational terms amounts to the same thing as building more submarines. Still, as American Enterprise Institute analyst Zack Cooper puts it, "the United States could essentially lose nearly one-tenth of its submarine fleet in the decade of its greatest need. Submarines are America's greatest asymmetric advantage over China, but this plan could cut three to five submarines out of the US force at a particularly critical time." The sale of the Virginia-class boats to Australia will require the approval of Congress, which, despite the strong support for AUKUS on Capitol Hill, may not want to wear this depletion of US SSN numbers.

These fateful decisions threaten to draw Australia into a war

What can we conclude?

For the last thirty years, the United States has maintained roughly the same amount of combat power in the Pacific. China has taken a far more central place in American national security strategy yet there is no sign of a radical change to American force structure in Asia, despite China's vastly expanded military capacity. Other than increasing its SSN commitment to the region, America's response to China's rise is not to assign more forces to Asia but to disperse its existing forces.

One way to interpret this evidence is that the US, far from redoubling its commitment to the defence of Taiwan and to its regional military superiority, is inching away from the objective of being able to defeat China militarily. In formal policy terms, the US is a long way from such a posture. Rhetorically, in fact, it is heading in the opposite direction. But the growing bipartisan political commitment to confronting China and defending Taiwan has never been reflected in US force structure in Asia. Gradually, and without ever formally deciding to do so, the US is drifting into a balance-of-power arrangement with China. Implicit in such an arrangement is that the US is giving up on the goal of defeating China in a conventional war and, yes, giving up on defending Taiwan. At some point, the reality of the situation will impose itself, and either US force structure or US rhetoric will have to change. Washington will have to drastically increase its regional combat power or reconcile itself to a more modest role in Asia's security architecture.

Australia has taken the decision to bring US combat forces, and its military strategy to fight China, onto our shores. We have also chosen to build military capabilities of our own that are designed expressly to contribute to American operations to defeat China. These fateful decisions threaten to draw Australia into a war that is not central to our security interests, and which could end in nuclear catastrophe. Yet America's reluctance to fully commit to military supremacy over China is a small blessing because it presents an opportunity for Australia to bend American objectives towards a more achievable and stabilising role of balancer rather than leader. That would be a sustainable objective for the US–Australia alliance, and a more justifiable basis on which the US could deploy forces to Australia. But as a military stronghold for a US effort to achieve regional dominance and defeat China in a war over Taiwan, Australia is materially eroding its security for no gain. ■

IMPERFECT UNION

Towards an alliance based on hope, not fear

Emma Shortis

Kevin Rudd is officially back. The former prime minister's return to state affairs – this time as Australia's ambassador to the United States – has been, by all accounts, well received in Washington. The appointment also, of course, raised a flurry of questions from the media, as Rudd always does. Alongside the one about his managerial style, and the one about whether he would undercut foreign minister Penny Wong, was another big one: what about his criticisms of that other former head of state, Donald Trump? How would those critiques (most of which were, appropriately, delivered on Twitter), along with Rudd's anti–News Corp campaign, affect his ability to conduct the apparently politically neutral job of alliance diplomacy? SBS News pointed out that Rudd had been an "outspoken critic" of Trump; *The Australian Financial Review* argued that his criticism was "a potential future problem ... that could become an issue". *The Sydney Morning*

Herald suggested that the possibility of "another colourful Republican" assuming power would be one of the "huge risks" of appointing Rudd.

On the same day as Rudd's appointment was announced, the congressional committee examining the former president's attempt to never leave the White House in the first place dropped its final report. In an unprecedented move, the House Select Committee on the January 6 Attack referred Trump for prosecution, recommending that the Department of Justice pursue him for, among other criminal charges, "inciting, assisting, aiding, or comforting an insurrection".

The juxtaposition of the coverage of Rudd's appointment with the House Select Committee's report revealed the ongoing inability, or unwillingness, of much of the mainstream media to grasp the gravity of the threat Trump and his followers pose to American democracy, and the possible implications of that threat for Australia.

The tone of the coverage implied, perhaps unwittingly, that it would be business as usual if Trump or someone just as "colourful" assumed the presidency. The "huge risk" of appointing an "outspoken critic" seemed to be that it might make life difficult for Rudd (and Australia) if he had to deal with a person who has been referred for criminal charges for attempting to stage a coup, who has since been indicted on other criminal charges, and who is still blithely talking about suspending the US Constitution.

The real risks lie in not facing the assumptions at play here. The obvious one is that Australia's security ties with the United States might be badly weakened if an incoming Trump or Trump-like administration, incensed by Rudd's criticisms, abandons Australia, leaving us exposed, weak and alone – and that such an outcome should be our biggest concern. The deeper assumption, fed by the fear that sits at the heart of the alliance, is that if Trump returns – however that might come about – the Australian government of the day would still need and want to tie the security of this country to that version of the United States.

Interests, values and the "capital-A Alliance"

In discussing the alliance, there is a tendency – inherited mostly from the disciplines of international relations and political science – to draw arbitrary lines between interests and values. One recent and important study of Australians' views of the alliance found that most apply a cost-benefit analysis to it: "Alliance supporters believe that the bedrock of the Alliance is shared interests, rather than shared values, or indeed a sense of shared history." The underlying concern about Rudd's appointment was that values were being placed above interests – that it was not in Australia's *interests* for him to have made those statements about *values* (in this case, democracy or, at a stretch, anti-fascism) because values are not the bedrock of the "capital-A Alliance"; *interests* (that is, security concerns) are.

The study – published through the United States Studies Centre (USSC) and funded by the Department of Defence's Strategic Policy Grants Program – asked important questions of people who don't usually get to talk about the alliance. It found:

> There is uncertainty among Australians about what the Alliance is for today, as distinct from what it is against, or what it has been in the past. The perceived lack of a sense of purpose in the Alliance is a common theme ... Most Australians are looking for articulation of a positive, more aspirational vision for the Alliance that they can subscribe to.

This unique study, alongside questions about Rudd's appointment, quietly revealed the confusion that lies at the heart of the modern alliance. What, exactly, is it *for*? Is it about security? Shared interests? Shared values? Or perhaps shared "convictions", as the Australian Minister for Defence, Richard Marles, has suggested?

Australians' "uncertainty" about the alliance reflects this confusion, or perhaps murkiness, around potential trade-offs between interests and values. When the current prime minister, Anthony Albanese, and the foreign minister, Penny Wong, speak about the alliance, they tend to tack closely to the "interests" side of the equation. In Albanese's initial meetings with US president Joe Biden, for example, their self-described focus was on shared interests – executing the AUKUS agreement, securing the Indo-Pacific and acting on climate. Questions of democracy and "shared values" didn't really come up.

But other people are talking about them. In July last year, Marles said that the alliance is "a unique and thriving project: driven not only by our nations' geopolitical interests, but also by our profound commitment to democracy, open economies, free and just societies".

In December, Marles' US counterpart, Secretary of Defense Lloyd Austin, agreed that the "bond between our democracies and our peoples has been forged by shared sacrifice, shared values, and shared history".

We know, loosely, what the alliance is against. We do not know what it is for. There's no reason that it cannot be about interests *and* values, after all: surely it is in our interests, as democracies, to defend our values of, well, democracy. So, shouldn't it have been a good thing – in fact, right and proper, even *necessary* – that Rudd roundly and loudly criticised an attempt by Republicans to destroy that shared foundational value? Isn't that in our shared interests too?

Some of the "uncertainty" around these questions stems from the fact that many Australians know the alliance isn't really "for" the shared value of democracy. It's not even clear that democracy could be described as a "value", though it is consistently described that way by leaders on both sides of the Pacific. Regardless, "interests" doesn't mean defending democracy per se, but hard-headed assessments of national security requirements. In President Biden's framing, the current strategic environment is about "democracies versus autocracies", but what he means by "democracy" in the international context is not the same as his understanding of "democracy" at home. Internationally, democracies line up against autocracies in defence of US hegemony and the "rules-based order", not in defence of democracy as a practice. An alliance built on the shared "value" of democracy would look very different to what we have now. As many historians have already pointed out, what the USSC study described as the "capital-A

Alliance" has been primarily focused on a fearful assessment of security interests. The creeping logic of national security was ingrained from the start. And in this country, that securitisation always manifests as anti-democratic.

The latest alliance development, AUKUS, was negotiated entirely in secret. Most members of the government that negotiated it didn't even know it was coming. The nuclear-powered revival of the Anglosphere was sprung on Australians without any kind of democratic consultation or debate. Decades of positive contributions to international disarmament, a proud history of anti-nuclear protest, and public sentiment overwhelmingly opposed to nuclear power and nuclear weapons were all dismissed overnight. Meanwhile, most Australians aren't permitted to know what happens at the joint facilities we host with the Americans. Our national security establishment has reacted with barely muted outrage at the suggestion that maybe, just maybe, the democratically elected and accountable parliament of this country should have some say in whether we once again follow the United States into war.

> **January 6 should have prompted a national reflection on the alliance**

These are not new arguments, and in fact the USSC study suggests that a large number of Australians are not particularly concerned about democratic accountability within the alliance specifically. There is a widely held belief, reflected in both the survey results and in opposition to war powers reform, that democratic accountability and decisions about national security aren't always compatible. The "capital-A Alliance" runs on that assumption, consistently doubling down on secrecy in the interests of security and against the "value" of democracy.

Australians surveyed by the USSC are aware that when it comes to the Alliance, security always trumps democracy (pun intended). If the Alliance understood democracy as a fundamental value, or even a core shared interest, then surely an Australian government would not have jettisoned its relationship with France – an important player in the Indo-Pacific, and the country that supported, more than any other, the United States' historic journey to democracy – in favour of further enmeshment with the "Anglosphere".

Prioritising this anti-democratic securitisation distorts the relationship between the internationally focused Alliance and domestic politics, assuming and sometimes insisting that the two operate independently of each other. Once again, many Australians see through these arbitrary distinctions between democracy at home and the way the idea is deployed internationally. The USSC study found that "Australians believe that stability in the Alliance will be dependent on domestic political developments in the US – including the potential erosion of democracy – rather than anything that may occur in Australia." They are entirely correct. But that sentiment isn't reflected in any official discussion of the Alliance. The dividing lines drawn between interests and values assume that defending democracy is always about looking out, never about looking in. While the Australian Department of Defence, for example, recognises that political instability presents a threat to regional security, it doesn't appear to extend that assessment to the US domestic context. The 2020 Defence Strategic Update noted that in Australia's strategic environment, "state fragility, exacerbated by governance and economic challenges, has the potential to facilitate threats to the region including the spread of terrorism and activities that undermine stability and sovereignty". The Strategic Update, and the vast majority of thinking and writing on the alliance, assumes that such "state fragility" happens in nations outside Australia's major security alliances, not within them.

January 6 should have shaken this assumption. It should have prompted a national reflection on the alliance and Australia's role in the world. It did not. But it is worth asking, again and again: what happens if Australia's security and the interests and values that underpin the US alliance – whether state fragility as a security threat or democracy as a shared value, take your pick – can no longer be reconciled?

What if?

Many Americans are themselves deeply worried about the integrity of their democracy. While the results of the November 2022 midterm elections might have assuaged some of that concern, the fear still exists, and it is legitimate. That is because evidence consistently shows there is a particular voting group that *isn't* concerned about democracy. In fact, quite the opposite. Among the headlines blasting statistics such as "One in three Americans believe violence against the government is justified" or "Two-fifths of Americans believe civil war likely in the next decade", fine-grained analysis gets lost. Dig deeper, and it becomes clear that more white Republicans believe both of these things than other demographic groups. A year after the insurrection, around 40 per cent of Republicans thought that violence against the government might be justified, compared to 23 per cent of Democrats. Put another way, 40 per cent of white Americans surveyed held this belief, compared to only 18 per cent of Black Americans.

That mid-2022 poll about the likelihood of civil war returned similar results. Over 50 per cent of Republicans – a demographic that overlaps with the most heavily armed parts of the population – thought civil war could occur in the next decade, compared to 40 per cent of Democrats and independents. In a country where there are 1.3 guns for every person, that's a pretty big reason for concern.

None of these statistics means that civil war is coming. They do suggest that escalating domestic political violence and its further normalisation is likely. That is already happening, and it may get worse. As the Irish writer Fintan O'Toole so clearly articulated in 2021 (writing about Ireland in the 1970s), "Premonitions of civil war served not as portents to be heeded, but as a warrant for carnage." A year later, the writer David Remnick described the United States as "a nation in a state of continuing crisis".

What are the implications of this continuing crisis, or a more successful coup attempt, for the rest of us? With a few important exceptions, there is startlingly little written – in Australia, internationally and even within the United States – on the "what if" question. Much of the US commentary is focused on the immediate ramifications of the insurrection, asking what might have happened if the mob had caught Vice President Mike Pence or Speaker Nancy Pelosi, or had managed to delay the certification of the election result. There is very little on what might have happened next – how the Pentagon would have responded, if the military might have intervened, or how the outgoing president might have reacted to a different outcome on the Capitol.

What are the implications of this continuing crisis?

Pondering these questions does feel, to be fair, as if we might be straying into the realm of speculative fiction, into an even more embarrassing version of *The Handmaid's Tale*. To again quote O'Toole, this risks repeating "[t]he comforting fiction that the U.S. used to be a glorious and settled democracy", thus "prevent[ing] any reckoning with the fact that its current crisis is not a terrible departure from the past but rather a product of the unresolved contradictions of its history". But that does *not* mean that speculation based on evidence and an understanding of American history cannot or should not be done (to take the literary equivalent further, we might attempt to channel Octavia Butler rather than Margaret Atwood).

There has been some conjecture about the impact that the collapse of American democracy could have on the rest of the world. This kind of analysis is familiar to historians of US foreign policy – mostly, hand-wringing about the blow to American credibility and a deep-seated fear that the shining light on the hill, the guidepost for and inspiration to aspiring democrats the world over, might be snuffed out. In mainstream media, at least, there does not appear to be much speculation about the real-world impact of such a downfall.

In Australia, some important thinking is happening about what Trump redux might mean for us. In the Lowy Institute's *The Interpreter*, for example, both Grant Wyeth and Ben Scott have attempted to answer this question. Scott outlined the links between Trumpian conspiracy theories about the "Deep State" and American conservatives' broader fixation on Australian Covid policy responses, arguing that Trump's return might mean a more aggressive "meddling in democracies such as Australia" alongside further efforts to strengthen and empower far-right networks internationally. The links between far-right networks and leaders in countries such as the United States, Brazil and Hungary bear this argument out. Similarly, Wyeth argued correctly that although no one in any official position will state it openly, "Maintenance of the two countries' shared values now relies on the Democratic Party being in power."

This work suggests that discussion about the alliance in Australia is broadening, as many have long called for (including in the pages of Australian Foreign Affairs). These interventions, however, tend to focus on the international arena – what the implications of Trump redux might be for the alliance, for Australia's national security in the context of US–China relations, and for US policy on the Indo-Pacific. They are, after all, writing about foreign affairs.

The "capital-A Alliance", however, has a significant physical presence on Australian domestic soil. To stray once again into speculation – as any good foreign policy must do in planning for the future – it is worth considering what a successful insurrection might have meant for Australia. Australia invests eye-watering amounts of money in defence contracts with the US government and private arms providers. What might happen to those contracts if there was a cataclysmic collapse in relations between the White House and the Pentagon? What would be the impact on the global economy? And if the insurrectionists had come across, for example, Vice President Mike Pence's backup nuclear "football", as they nearly did, what would such a colossal security breach mean for Australia, given this nation's deep integration into US military structures? Or another example: what if a hostile foreign government got access to highly classified documents about AUKUS and nuclear integration because a president had removed them illegally from the White House?

To take these questions even further: how might an Australian government respond if, to use the words of President Biden, "semi-fascists" were suddenly in charge of the greatest military power in the world? Who would those 2000 US marines on rotation in Darwin answer to? How would they respond to events at home?

What would we do if our best friend in the world, our great protector, descended into a violent fascist dictatorship?

These are extreme hypotheticals. But two years ago, we were very close to having to respond to them in the real world. The danger of that happening again is also real. Trump and the unresolved contradictions of US history have hardly gone away. And if they manage to come roaring back to power, they will turn the alliance on its head. The question might be, then, not the usual "What if they abandon us?" but "What if they don't?"

There is no question that the current government would respond to a Trump or Trump-like administration, or even another attempted insurrection (successful or otherwise), very differently to the previous one. Its appointment of Rudd makes that clear. What is not clear, at least from the outside, is how it might be *able* to respond to such events or where the red lines would be.

Australia is well practised at establishing diplomatic relationships with non-democratic governments, something that is essential to the maintenance of regional and global stability and security. But it is uncertain how such a relationship might be built with a dramatically different United States. Would a Labor government – or any government – be able to extract Australia from arrangements such as Force Posture or Pine Gap? Or, to ask a more uncomfortable question, is it possible that it might decide not to try? That it might make the decision implied by those questions about Rudd's appointment – that Australia should always rely on a US security blanket, even if its threads were no longer held together by shared systems of government? Or that insulating or extracting ourselves would simply be impossible, leaving us trapped with a foreign and security policy premised on interoperability and interchangeability with a violently unhinged autocracy?

To those sceptical of the alliance, or already opposed to it, the answers to these questions – and to any alliance developments – would presumably be that Australia needs to build a more independent foreign and security policy, to shore up its sovereignty, particularly in defence materiel, or even to abandon the alliance together. For the most part, and for now, at least, those options seem politically impossible; while there are calls from the Greens and the broader peace and anti-nuclear movements to do so, and increasing attention is being paid to those ideas, there is no appetite within the parties of government or the mainstream media for even considering such options. Such calls also get unfairly trapped into binaries that dismiss the good things about the relationship – a shared history of democratic government, of course, but more importantly a shared history of democratic solidarity between peoples that have built international coalitions to oppose apartheid, labour exploitation, racist policing and environmental destruction. The bonds, in short, between two imperfect democracies, and not the bonds between an empire and its deputy sheriff.

We sit in a rare historical moment

It should be possible to answer these pressing questions about the future of the alliance without falling into tired binaries of abandonment versus subservience. We sit in a rare historical moment, marked by a willingness among Australians to rethink or reshape the relationship. It is a moment that should be seized before it disappears again. While polling consistently shows broad support for the alliance, the recent USSC study shows that there is room to move. Many Australians are hoping for the "articulation of a positive, more aspirational vision" of the relationship.

With the United States embroiled in continuing crisis, developing and articulating such a vision becomes ever more urgent. Doing so might help to ensure that the alliance (and the rest of the world) minimises the fallout from the worst-case scenarios of US democratic decline or collapse. For the current Australian government, it also offers an opportunity to seize the likely narrow window of opportunity to rethink other less extreme but no less uncomfortable realities: the ever-present risk of bad American decision-making and the violent exercise of US power in service of such decisions. This is especially important in light of what Kishore Mahbubani recently described as "the most fundamental political reality of our time: that the era of western domination is ending".

Transitioning the alliance

Domestically, both President Biden and Prime Minister Albanese were elected on programs of gentle progressive change, especially on climate. There remains an appetite among those who elected them for a positive and aspirational approach to climate action, addressing racial and gender injustice and reducing economic inequality. They were elected, in short, on platforms of transition.

Both leaders have embarked on such programs, in their own ways. In mid-2022, Biden oversaw the passage of the *Inflation Reduction Act*, a mammoth piece of legislation that, despite significant flaws, is the largest and potentially most important piece of climate legislation in American history. At almost the same time, the Albanese government oversaw the passage of its own climate laws, locking in emissions-reduction targets. Both have pursued policies that are explicitly and unapologetically designed to support women through, for example, childcare reform. And both governments are acknowledging, and listening to, Indigenous voices. One of Biden's first executive orders cancelled the Keystone XL fossil pipeline project. In both countries, for the first time in our shared histories, Indigenous women have been appointed to key ministries. At the end of 2022, Biden hosted the first in-person Tribal Nations Summit in six years. The Albanese government will, at long last, hold a referendum on the Indigenous Voice to Parliament.

From a genuinely progressive perspective, all of this is too slow and none of it is anywhere near enough. But it is, potentially, a platform on which something new might be built, and at least recognises that functioning democracies require genuine, sustained and inclusive participation. Successful transition, especially when it comes to the climate, depends on it.

As yet, this transition agenda has not infiltrated the "capital-A Alliance". Shallow talk of extending the alliance to cover the shared interest of acting on climate only draws focus away from the need for coordinated, progressive global action (as opposed to exclusive bi- or trilateral partnerships) while further securitising climate risks. That securitisation and compartmentalisation is, predictably, both anti-democratic and inadequate. Even setting aside the catastrophic environmental risks of nuclear power and weapons, none of the talk of broadening the Alliance to include joint climate action will acknowledge, let alone address, the fact that, according to *Nature*, "if they were a nation, US forces would have the highest per-capita emissions in the world". A securitised climate agenda, run mostly by two defence departments, will continue to see climate change as a security problem, not a political or an economic one. It sees the large-scale displacement of people as a threat to security and stability, not as a political and moral responsibility to be handled with empathy. An alliance founded in the "crucible of war", as defence minister Richard Marles put it recently, has no interest in a progressive, democratically accountable transition. It is actively oriented against one.

None of this is inevitable. The alliance, just like our domestic politics, could transition into something quite different. Arguably, it is only through such a transition – one that shifts the "capital-A Alliance" from its anti-democratic national security agenda to one based on shared progressive values – that the relationship will be built on the "positive, more aspirational vision" so many people in both places crave, for their homes and for the roles their nations play in the world.

Basing the relationship on those bonds, rather than on cold, anti-democratic assessments of security, does not mean setting security aside; far from it. It would mean understanding security differently. The domestic understanding of security that Biden and Albanese appear to share – one based on reducing environmental, racial and economic inequalities and ensuring active, sustained participation in healthy democracies – could and should apply to the international arena. The alliance and its architecture, in concert with the long list of acronyms into which the relationship has expanded, could more closely align its ambition to the domestic visions of its component national governments. Leaders of each country might attempt to unite their domestic and their international selves, and in more than just rhetoric. For the Australian government, this would mean always seeking out, encouraging and supporting the Biden who passed the *IRA* for the good of the American people, and not the Biden who is running a global empire. It would mean an alliance based on democratic *solidarity*, not on shallow and inauthentic democracy promotion. Such a relationship would understand democracy as both shared interest and shared value, and as foundational to a sustainable and peaceful future.

It would mean an alliance based on democratic *solidarity*

This reframing of international security would lead to a very different understanding of potential threats and how to mitigate them.

The foundational document of the alliance, the ANZUS Treaty, was constructed with a particular, and deeply racist, view of outside threats as constant and inevitable. A values-based approach might challenge such assumptions at the heart of the alliance, leading to a foreign and security policy that aims, always, to avoid wars rather than assuming it will be necessary to fight them.

An understanding of the history of international relations that does not centre the United States shows that this is possible. At the same time that the ANZUS Treaty was being signed, European nations that had been engaged in centuries of existential conflict were beginning a long process of integration and collaboration. Openness to such possibilities in this part of the world could lead to more proactive policy developments and a shift from an almost exclusive focus on bi- and trilateral relationships with countries far outside our neighbourhood, to genuine collaboration in and with the region. This would mean, too, greater openness to all partners operating in the region: to Pacific nations, France, the European Union and New Zealand. While Australia of course already works with these "partners", they remain second in line behind the United States (if that wasn't obvious before 2021, AUKUS has made it abundantly clear).

A genuine reckoning with the "capital-A Alliance", through the lens of shared democratic values, must mean a reduction in aggressive "forward defence" acquisition. It should mean a slow, deliberate military extraction from the United States; not a total withdrawal, by any means, but small changes that might mean less "interoperability" and "interchangeability" and something less subject to the whims of the US empire. A smaller, adaptive defence force with a focus on peace-building and crisis response would greatly disrupt the escalation of threats encouraged by a posture of "forward defence", and help to end the fiction of nuclear deterrence. Reduced spend on the instruments of forward defence would also free up funding for progressive programs of climate action and poverty reduction, which governments across the Pacific have recognised as critical to security. In the event of a change of government in either nation, an alliance already in the process of transition might be less subject to hijacking by anti-democratic, war-mongering security interests.

Such a radically different future might be achieved through a patch-work of changes, slowly stitched together. Practically, such a patchwork could include policy initiatives in which values *inform* interests, rather than the other way around. Such initiatives already happen in the domestic context; there is no reason they could not be expanded internationally. Before the November 2022 midterms, for example, President Biden met in the White House with a group of pre-eminent US historians, who proceeded to warn him about the existential risks facing American democracy. It wasn't the first time he had consulted with historians, and it is unlikely to be the last. What might an international version of that meeting look like? Support for cooperation and consultation between experts on democracy might come, for example, through an expanded fellowship program run through the Quadrilateral Security Dialogue. The existing program, announced in 2021, is limited to graduates in the fields of science, technology, engineering and mathematics; there are no places for the humanities. For an alliance premised on the inevitability of war, whose remit has broadened from ANZUS to the Quad and now the forward-defence posture of AUKUS, it makes sense to only include disciplines that have invented new and more efficient ways to kill people. For an alliance focused on employing new technologies and scientific research to support a just and democratic climate transition, it does not. An expanded humanities fellowship program might begin to disrupt the Australian national security landscape, elevating research that doesn't rely on funding from defence departments or contractors that profit from conflict or the fear of it. With adequate support, such a program might build personal, professional and cross-institutional networks that rival those far-right networks already spanning the world – the ones that support insurrection attempts in Brazil, that have supportive global media empires doing week-long laudatory showcases on Hungary's far-right government, or that encourage white men to massacre.

On a grander scale, an alliance that connected our shared domestic politics to the ways our two nations behave in the world might also consider the implications of an Indigenous Voice to Parliament for foreign and security policy. How might such a critical development in the history of this nation change predominant understandings of the Alliance? Might that be an avenue for transitioning the alliance from a relationship based on fear to one based on collective security and peacebuilding? As James Blackwell and Julie Ballangarry have argued, Australia should build "a foreign policy which is inclusive of First Nations peoples and their knowledges". For that to happen,

> First Nations peoples require genuine participation and engagement which will only be achieved when we have a legitimate seat at the table where our voices are equal to those who sit beside us. This is the exact type of solution that a First Nations Voice enshrined in the Constitution, as envisioned by the Uluru Statement from the Heart, was designed to facilitate.

Building on important work already happening in the Department of Foreign Affairs and Trade, led by Wong, a foreign policy that genuinely included First Nations voices would approach the Indo-Pacific very differently. Centring millennia of knowledge and practice of collective security might engender, for example, a radically different approach to climate action and ocean governance. Agreements like the Treaty on the Prohibition of Nuclear Weapons – itself born of the leadership of Indigenous peoples – would need to be reconciled with AUKUS. Rather than dancing around the treaty for fear of upsetting the Alliance, Australia might move from abstention to champion and play a critical role in international threat-reduction and peacebuilding.

None of this precludes Australia from, in the words of Wong, having to "deal with the world as it is". But efforts "to shape it for the better" require radical courage, and radical hope. An alliance in transition might allow us to ask ourselves perhaps the most pressing question of all: what could we bring to the world if we weren't so afraid? ■

THE VIEW FROM AMERICA

We're still your best bet

Michael J. Green

America's leaders have found different ways to emphasise that a world absent US leadership is a world that its friends and allies would not want to see. Former secretary of state Madeleine Albright, whose Czech family had survived Hitler's Reich and Stalin's Soviet bloc, passionately called the United States "the indispensable nation". President Joe Biden likes to say that nobody has ever won by betting against America. Perhaps the most memorable example was that of the British foreign secretary Lord Carrington, who reportedly responded to his European counterparts' litany of complaints about the Reagan administration in the 1980s by acknowledging, "yes … yes … everything you say about the Americans is true … *but they're the only Americans we have*."

American capacity and resolve have formed the foundation of an Indo-Pacific order that has allowed Australia to thrive economically and geopolitically. It began with Franklin Roosevelt's decision after

Japan's 1941 attack on Pearl Harbor that the highest strategic priority in the Pacific was to stop Japan from cutting off Australia. Instead of retreating in the face of North Korea's Soviet-backed attack on South Korea in 1950, the United States formed the most powerful network of alliances and forward military presence the region had ever seen. When the Vietnam War threatened to weaken the American-led order, Nixon opened a new relationship with China to reset the balance of power. And in response to China's military expansion after the Cold War, the United States doubled-down on its alliance with Japan and launched a new partnership with India to sustain the region's favourable equilibrium. Over this same period, the US share of global economic output dropped from half to less than a quarter, but the American-led system largely endured because Washington successfully harnessed alliances, built economic rules and opened strategic relationships with former adversaries.

For US allies, of course, this history was not free from friction or anxiety about America's choices. When ANZUS was signed in 1951, the Pentagon rejected initial Australian requests for a greater concentration of US military power Down Under and focused on Japan and Korea instead. In the early 1960s, Robert Menzies argued with President Lyndon Johnson that US intervention was necessary to stop communism in South-East Asia, and then a decade later Gough Whitlam and Nixon fought with what historian James Curran calls "unholy fury" about American overcommitment in Vietnam. Nixon's subsequent withdrawal from South-East Asia under the "Guam

Doctrine" and then Jimmy Carter's attack on Asian allies over human rights rattled American partners, even prompting Seoul to begin a clandestine nuclear weapons program. In the 1980s, the US alliance with New Zealand broke over nuclear ship visits, while Americans told pollsters they saw Japan's economy as a greater threat than Soviet nuclear weapons. When the Clinton administration came into office cutting defence spending and picking trade and human rights fights with China, Japan and South-East Asia, the prominent Japanese journalist Yoichi Funabashi warned in the American version of *Foreign Affairs* that American leadership was over and the next century would bring the "Asianization of Asia". This was not the first or last such prediction. There has not been a decade since 1945 when editorials somewhere in Asia did not raise alarm about American reliability and staying power.

With the Trump presidency, the January 6 storming of the US Capitol and relentless stories about gun violence and political polarisation, these doubts are back in the public discourse. Biden's 2020 election victory and the defeat of election-denying extremist candidates in the 2022 midterms helped to restore confidence in American democracy and internationalism, but the subsequent fights over Kevin McCarthy's speakership and the national debt – and yet more stories of gun violence – suggest continued ills. And just as Soviet military expansionism or Japanese economic hyperpower seemed to amplify the weaknesses in American society in previous decades, today China looms large.

Yet as Carrington argued, these are the only Americans we have. It is easy enough to criticise American politics or society, which provide continuous grist for the critic's mills. And no criticism of America is more probing than that by Americans themselves: one is unlikely to find negative stories about the United States in *The Guardian, The Sydney Morning Herald* or News Corp that have not already surfaced on MSNBC, in *The New York Times* or on Fox News. When the US Studies Centre asked Australians about the state of democracy in America before the 2022 midterm election, half said they had concerns – but they were outnumbered by the 70 per cent of Americans who said *they* were concerned. However, the story of American democracy and society is almost always more complex than the headlines can convey. The current political polarisation is severe, yet every recent generation has been more progressive than the last. Polls show that younger Americans today are poised to be even more progressive and inclusive, and that Americans – especially younger Americans – retain a robust commitment to international engagement. And significantly, American leadership in the world is still based on a political system and national security institutions that are designed to accommodate criticism and direction from allies, who are increasingly important to American strategy.

So while the debate about America can and should continue, the question for Australia (and other allies) is not whether to abandon America – a choice rejected in polls and bipartisan policies. The critical question is what kind of America Australia needs – and what Canberra can do with other like-minded states to shape American strategy in ways that underpin Australian sovereignty and security.

Competing with China

One of the ironies of Washington these days is that amid the greatest political polarisation of a generation, there has never been more bipartisan consensus on policy towards the Indo-Pacific. This journey took a while. Every US president after the Cold War premised their approach to the world on the assertion that more would unite us with China than divide us, while hedging in case they were wrong. This combination of engaging and balancing was not always elegant, with senior officials often unsure which to emphasise. Clinton flirted with a "strategic partnership" with Beijing at the end of his term, which George W. Bush criticised, yet Bush then chose to attend the 2008 Beijing Olympics as a sign of goodwill to Chinese leader Hu Jintao. Barack Obama's administration initially thought it could cement trust with China by working together on global issues such as climate change, then swung towards countering China with the "pivot to Asia" in 2011; then back to engagement with talk of accepting Xi Jinping's "New Model of Great Power Relations" in 2013; and then finally back to confrontation after Xi militarised the South China Sea with three massive artificial island bases in 2014–15.

Donald Trump's 2017 "National Security Strategy" stated with characteristic crudeness that the US would henceforth treat China and Russia as strategic competitors. By that point, few leaders in Washington were prepared to disagree. Today, while the tone is different, there is enormous continuity on Asia policy from Trump to Biden. The Trump administration embraced Japanese prime minister Shinzo

Abe's proposal for a "Free and Open Indo-Pacific", a reconstituted US–Australia–Japan–India "Quad", and enhanced military capacity among close allies to deter China. Biden has redoubled these initiatives and added more, while largely rejecting Trump's destructive fantasies about escalating trade wars and withdrawing US troops from South Korea and NATO. The Biden administration's 2022 "Indo-Pacific Strategy" is the most coherent framework Washington has yet produced on the region and enjoys strong bipartisan support. That strategy argues that instead of attempting to shape Beijing's choices through *direct* engagement, the United States should prioritise shaping the region *around* China in order to blunt growing Chinese coercion and mercantilism. And it depends entirely on US allies and partners.

There has never been more bipartisan consensus on policy towards the Indo-Pacific

Indeed, this strategy is the greatest American investment in alliances since at least the 1980s. Through the AUKUS agreement, the United States has committed to transfer one of the crown jewels of American military technology – nuclear propulsion – to Australia. Only Britain enjoyed such a guarantee and that was back in 1957 at a time when British nuclear technology was already quite advanced. Where previous administrations might have balked at Japan's ambitions to deploy new weapons capable of striking adversaries, the Biden and Trump administrations have been fully supportive. India, too, is benefiting from expansive American expertise and equipment. And while Biden will be judged harshly by historians for the administration's chaotic withdrawal from Afghanistan, he will be rightly praised for his efforts to forge an international coalition to punish Vladimir Putin for his brutal invasion of Ukraine. That coalition has obvious implications for the Indo-Pacific, where Beijing will have noticed the power of global US alliances to punish aggressors.

The Biden administration also racked up a major success with allies when it reached agreement with Japan and the Netherlands in January 2023 to deny China access to the most advanced semiconductor fabrication technologies. This coalition responded to Beijing's ambitions to dominate artificial intelligence by ensuring that the democracies retain their lead in semiconductor production. This is not mere rent-seeking mercantilism: artificial intelligence will eventually shape everything from the battlefield to fundamental personal liberties. Multiple governments now agree that Xi Jinping's China – in which decreasing political freedoms at home is coupled with "wolf-warrior" diplomacy overseas – must not be allowed to dominate the information technologies of the future. Nor does the US technology strategy represent economic containment, since trade has not been seriously impacted. Indeed, the recent US Studies Centre survey found a convergence of American and Australian public views that economic and technological dependence on China must be reduced, but economic engagement overall should continue.

While policy debates in Washington are always ugly up close, the Biden administration, in spite of the polarisation, has demonstrated the kind of strategic competence that allowed previous American governments to preserve a favourable regional order in the face of hegemonic challengers. China is a bigger challenge than Japan or the Soviet Union were last century, but it also has big internal problems. Xi Jinping is presiding over a government that is suppressing innovation and the private sector, encouraging technology decoupling by other economies with his strategies such as "dual circulation", and provoking antagonism with aggressive policies in every direction except towards Russia. The birthrate in China has halved over the past five years – something demographers see only during times of catastrophe, such as the Great Leap Forward or a world war – indicating that not everything is right with the Chinese people. Few economists still predict that China will surpass the United States to become the world's top economy by the 2030s. This internal uncertainty and weakness should make us wary of projections of a straight upward trajectory of Chinese power.

Doing the wrong things first

Winston Churchill is credited (mistakenly) with saying, "You can count on the Americans to do all the wrong things first before they do the right thing." With its alliance-centric strategy, the Biden administration is doing the most basic things right – but also doing some important things wrong.

First, the American political enthusiasm for competing with China has crowded out some of the nuance that allies need to see in US–China relations. Ultimately, public sentiment in the United States is not so different from that in Australia or Japan, with polls showing majorities are distrustful of China, favour like-minded allies, support protection of core technologies and oppose complete economic containment of China. But the arms race in Washington on China policy is more intense than in Tokyo or Canberra (let alone in Brussels or Singapore) and the Biden administration is struggling to find the right rhetorical balance. After long internal debates about how to characterise the floor under US–China relations, the White House settled on awkward phrasing in its 2022 "National Security Strategy", asserting that "peaceful coexistence with China is not impossible". Aside from sounding like it was written by Dr Spock from *Star Trek,* the double negatives and Chinese terms such as "peaceful coexistence" reflect an unresolved conceptual and political tension in the strategy.

This is not to argue that Beijing eagerly awaits cooperation with Washington. Beijing is rebuffing US efforts to work together on North Korea, climate change and even illegal Chinese shipments of Fentanyl, a drug responsible for the deaths of hundreds of young Americans. As foreign minister Penny Wong acknowledged in her speech to the National Press Club, President Biden has also tried without success to win Beijing's support for putting "guardrails" around strategic competition. There should be more US–China dialogue and cooperation in all these areas, but Xi's government is demanding concessions Americans will not make on issues ranging from Taiwan to human rights and is backing those demands with a massive anti-American social mobilisation campaign within China and disinformation campaigns abroad. Beijing did not formerly link issues in this way – an approach more characteristic of North Korea's diplomatic playbook or the early years of Mao's China. Nevertheless, the Biden administration would do well to articulate a clearer vision for more productive relations with China – as Australia, Japan and Korea have, despite their friction with Beijing. This would ease cooperation with countries worried about entrapment in an American strategy of regime change and reassure allies unnerved by the whiff of hawkish panic in some of Washington's recent rhetoric about China.

Thus, as Theodore Roosevelt would put it, the United States must learn to speak softly and carry a big stick. Making sure the United States has that big stick is a second area where the Biden administration still has work to do. The US military has lost its air and sea dominance over China in the Western Pacific, but Beijing will continue to face an existential risk if it invades Taiwan or attacks Japan in the era of global economic interdependence and nuclear weapons. The US Navy retains a significant lead over China in key areas such as undersea warfare but investment in deterrence and allied capability are critical to suppressing Beijing's ambitions. Biden is the first Democratic Party candidate since Lyndon Johnson to campaign on increasing defence spending, and postwar Republican-led Houses have always supported larger military budgets, but the legislation authorising those increases has yet to be implemented.

The third mistake Biden is making is to tolerate the same protectionist impulses Trump campaigned on. The US system in the Indo-Pacific has always been strongest when it rested on a combination of alliances, deterrence and market-opening trade agreements that expanded the community of like-minded states in the region. This was not always an area of perfect harmony for Canberra and Washington either. During World War II, Australian Labor governments fought against American demands to cut tariffs as a condition for lend lease. After the Hawke government embraced free trade, the position was reversed, and Washington found itself trying to keep up with Canberra's enthusiasm for open markets. But even with these mismatches, both capitals have seen an ambitious trade policy as essential to the security and prosperity of the region.

The high-water mark was the Trans-Pacific Partnership (TPP), which Trump withdrew from in his first week as president. Biden's team came into office in 2021 terrified of trade politics in the swing states of Pennsylvania, Michigan and Ohio. The most the administration has been able to do to fill the vacuum has been to launch the Indo-Pacific Economic Framework (IPEF). Japan and Australia have gamely championed IPEF as useful for addressing issues such as supply chain security and digital trade, alongside countries not originally in TPP, such as India and Indonesia. Those claims are true, but IPEF has none of the agenda-setting power provided by all previous US trade agreements in the region. And so Canberra, Tokyo, Wellington and others are quietly searching for ways to nudge Washington back to more substantive trade strategies.

The administration also still has to fix the wiring of American alliances. To build submarines and other advanced capabilities under AUKUS, for example, Australia will need thousands of approvals from the US State Department – approvals that threaten to derail the entire effort. Washington's export control rules were originally designed to keep the best technologies away from China and Russia, but now they are harming US allies. This is on Biden's radar, but decades of inertia behind American arms control and technology transfer rules continue to confound Canberra. This is not just an American problem. Australia will also have to upgrade its workforce and protection of technology, and probably make further increases in defence spending to build the deterrence capabilities promised in agreements such as AUKUS.

These challenges no doubt frustrate officials in defence or DFAT – and no less so in the Pentagon and State Department. But they pale in comparison with some of the discord and fury of previous spats between Washington and Canberra. Meanwhile, polls show that US allies and partners want more cooperation with the United States, not less. The major democracies are moving closer together – from AUKUS to the Quad – and this has led to agreements that get less attention in Australia, such as the new US–Japan Defence Guidelines, the Philippines' extension of access to US military forces, South Korea's Indo-Pacific Strategy or NATO's focus on China in its new Strategic Concept. To be sure, in large swaths of South Asia and South-East Asia, the Middle East, Latin America and Sub-Saharan Africa the picture is more mixed. At times, Beijing has gained ground through the Belt and Road Initiative and effective disinformation campaigns,

None of the successful states in the region are betting against America

while at other times its heavy-handed military and diplomatic pressure have backfired. Most of South-East Asia and the Pacific want to avoid being caught in the great-power game. Their focus is on preserving sovereignty – and that explains why Australia, the United States and especially Japan are trusted more than China across Asia, which views Xi's call for a "Community of Common Destiny" as eerily reminiscent of Japan's Greater East Asia Co-Prosperity Sphere. That contest for influence in South-East Asia and the Pacific will continue, but to use Joe Biden's phrase, none of the successful states in the region are betting against America.

The *Hamilton* theory of American dysfunction

The most visible manifestation of trouble in America in recent times has probably been Trump and Trumpism. Trump's version of populism, nativism and quasi-authoritarianism reflects a phenomenon that has, for the most part, spared Australia while sweeping over democracies in much of the rest of the globe. In the US, this populism, matched at times by extremism on the far left, has collected in tide pools created by gerrymandered Congressional districts and the profitable "angertainment" of cable television. As scholars such as E.J. Dionne have pointed out, these tide pools would not exist if the United States, like Australia, had compulsory voting, which would force candidates to play for support in the middle. For now, Americans are unlikely to embrace compulsory voting – though some states are instituting the next best solution, which is rank preference voting. Meanwhile, as Kevin

McCarthy found when he was struggling to get votes as Speaker of the House, there will continue to be safe spaces for politicians running on populism over principle, publicity over policy, and nihilistic destruction over consensus and national interest.

But is this a trend? Anyone who has watched the musical *Hamilton* knows that muckraking character assassination and polarisation have been features of American politics since Hamilton and Jefferson clashed in George Washington's first cabinet meeting. Moreover, the 2022 midterm election was a repudiation of election-denying extremism in every race other than J.D. Vance's Senate election in Ohio, though the hedge fund executive turned Trump supporter significantly underperformed other Republicans in his home state. Trump's star is nowhere near as bright as it once was, with majorities of Americans saying they do not want him to run in the 2024 election; former allies declaring he is unelectable; and multiple lawsuits under way against him.

Then there is the question about social progress in the United States writ large. Many Australians were appalled at the US Supreme Court's recent decision to overturn the constitutional right to abortion or the inability of Congress to pass effective gun control legislation in the wake of mass shootings. Polls show that a majority of Americans agree. But the larger American experiment to create "a more perfect union" has achieved changes in politics and society that would have stunned earlier generations. By way of perspective, Americans in polls are far more likely to eschew racist attitudes than Australians, while American cabinets have long been the most multicultural of any in the

G20, including Australia (though in recent years Canada has set the standard). There is a real possibility that the 2024 presidential election could be a contest between two candidates of colour, with popular Republican senator Tim Scott of South Carolina taking on Vice President Kamala Harris or another rising star such as Maryland governor Wes Moore. American debates about race and democracy are more visible, vocal and vociferous – and sometimes violent – but adversaries who mistake those fights as signs of decline and not also as acts of renewal risk falling into what Robert Kagan calls in his new book "the America trap".

Finally, there is the question of how much the polarised social and cultural debates in America bear on its actual leadership in the world. The humorist Mark Twain famously said that the music of Richard Wagner is "not as bad as it sounds". The rhetoric of politicians such as Trump, Republican congressman Matthew Gaetz or Democrat Ilhan Omar certainly sounds bad but does not reflect the large majorities in both parties who rallied in support of Ukraine or AUKUS. When Trump, as president, flirted with pulling troops out of South Korea, senators from his own party quietly introduced legislation requiring Congressional approval. These were not just the anachronistic rearguard actions of a handful of out-of-touch elites. Polls by the US Studies Centre, the Centre for Strategic and International Studies, Gallup, the Chicago Council on Global Affairs and others show that the American public's support for international economic engagement, defending allies such as Australia and standing up to dictators is as high as it has ever been. This is not just idealism but well-considered self-interest. When, in late 2022, the US Studies Centre asked Americans if alliances make America safer, the number who answered yes jumped fourteen points from the year before to 58 per cent as the public watched what was happening in Ukraine and the Taiwan Strait.

The risk is not a return to isolationism but rather that polarised politics lead to self-inflicted wounds as members of Congress play high-risk games of chicken around the debt ceiling or the nomination of key officials. Dysfunction was built into the system of checks and balances from the beginning of the Republic. It is a system that allows the American people to take the lead in innovation, renovation and renewal, but it can produce divisiveness and suboptimal policy along the way.

America remains the indispensable power despite itself

The only Americans we have

What, then, is a close US ally like Australia to do? There is no indication that Labor or the Coalition are going to choose neutrality or distancing from America – not with Chinese coercive pressure a new reality and other close partners such as Japan and South Korea choosing to reinforce the American alliance system rather than defect. America remains the indispensable power despite itself. In a world without US leadership, Putin would today be ruling Ukraine through proxies in

Kyiv, Taipei might have succumbed to Chinese coercion, and corporations would depend on China's increasingly predatory economic model for growth, without the alternative provided by an open and innovative American economy.

Hedging against uncertainty about America may seem a sensible choice for Australia and would likely not collide with Washington's expectations of Canberra when one considers how it would look. An extreme hedging option for Australia would be to pursue independent nuclear weapons. However, there would be no public support, a dangerous regional backlash and a significant weakening of deterrence already provided by US nuclear weapons. A more logical and subtle hedging strategy would be to pursue sovereign military capabilities designed for the defence of Australia. At the top of the list would be guided weapons and high-end attack submarines. Defence Minister Richard Marles has emphasised that these capabilities are essential to secure Australian sovereignty in a more dangerous geopolitical environment – and that the alliance with the United States is essential to obtaining them. The United States provides the best and most advanced kit with the most reliable supply for any geopolitical threat Australia would face. The road to sovereign defence capabilities goes through the alliance, in other words, and the complexities of tech transfer notwithstanding, the United States is all in for helping Australia get there.

Another logical hedging strategy would be to enhance security cooperation with Japan, India and other middle powers such as Korea. Such moves – the security agreement prime ministers Albanese and

Kishida signed in Perth in October 2022 is an example – have been warmly welcomed in Washington. For some time, the US has encouraged bilateral alliances within Asia to shore up regional order and deterrence. Once again, Australia does not face a choice between the alliance or Asia – it is a natural complementarity.

Australia's most important unfinished task may be to shape choices in Washington. Americans think alliances are more important than ever and Australia has almost unparalleled access, influence and respect in DC. Australian officials and scholars are embedded in the Pentagon, the State Department, think tanks and universities, at higher levels than any ally other than the UK (and more than the UK in agencies and research institutes focused on the Indo-Pacific). The history of going in harm's way together since the Battle of Hamel in 1918 still tugs on the conscience of senior American officials, while the Five Eyes intelligence relationship allows levels of information-sharing that far surpass what is possible with Japan or South Korea. Importantly, Australian diplomats and political leaders usually take their disagreements with US policy inside in order to align with like-minded officials or members of Congress and increase the chances of a favourable outcome. Some governments – the French and German, for example – will often posture against the United States for domestic political reasons. As a result, they are far less effective in shaping American decisions. Of course, the Australian approach opens officials to criticism from the left that Canberra is not more vocal in its disagreements with America, but managing the US alliance matters politically in Australia more than it does in Europe – as Labor leader Mark Latham found in 2004 after he tried to wave the anti-American card.

One critical area of coordination will be China strategy. It would be a colossal mistake for Australian officials or politicians to lecture their American counterparts on China, as I observed during my time serving in the government. Australia is not more economically intimate with China: US trade with China is more than five times Australia's and spans more sectors of the economy, even if Australia's relative dependence on China for exports is higher. While Australia has outstanding China scholars (Bates Gill of the Asia Society and Richard McGregor of the Lowy Institute would be at the top of the list), the American government, think tanks, universities and businesses are populated by hundreds if not thousands of experts fluent in Mandarin and well connected in China. Australia is not necessarily smarter on China; it is just that America's China debate is more unruly.

Australian discussions with the United States should focus on achieving specific outcomes. An obvious place to start is trade policy. There are many constituents within the United States – from farmers and ranchers to big business and the national security community – who are frustrated with the trade impasse since the US withdrawal from TPP. The politics are topsy-turvy, with Republican interest groups such as agriculture and big business supporting trade but rank-and-file voters sceptical, while Democratic interest groups such as trade unions are sceptical of trade and more cosmopolitan rank-and-file Democratic voters are in favour. It is difficult to say when and how these convoluted politics will sort themselves out, but Australia, Japan and others have a big stake. Frankly, Washington seems exhausted by trade politics, and US allies would do well to keep injecting urgency back into the debate.

The mechanics of Australia's alliance with the United States will require painstaking and often dreary bureaucratic work, but this must be done for US export controls to move into the new era of strategic competition. There are creative ways to open the channels of technology transfer – for example, through US presidential executive orders that would carve out AUKUS – but these will require Australia to do its part to adjust policies in places and otherwise reassure Washington. Other big decisions are coming down the pike. If the US leases attack submarines to the Royal Australian Navy, for example, how will the joint crews be commanded in the event of a contingency? As China's missiles bring Australia into range – the first such territorial threat since the Cold War and really since World War II – how will Australia and the United States modernise cooperation on nuclear strategy and extended deterrence? In the past, Australia assumed there would be ten years before these issues had to be sorted out for the defence of Australia against direct attack. The government's recent Defence Strategic Review now predicates that warning time is essentially zero. On the Korean peninsula,

The founding fathers vowed to create a more perfect union – they did not claim they had one

and for NATO, the joint and combined command relationships were built precisely because there would be no warning time before the Warsaw Pact or North Korea struck. Australia is not likely to form a comparable command with the United States even in the current geopolitical climate, but decision-making will have to be more agile and intimate. Whatever the new arrangements, there will have to be analysis and debate by parliament, Congress and the public. Interestingly, for a long time, the US–Australia alliance did not rely on the kind of think tank forums to facilitate such debates, unlike the US–Japan, US–Korea or trans-Atlantic alliances. That is changing with the new presence in Washington of the Australian Strategic Policy Institute, the establishment of the Australia Chair at the Center for Strategic and International Studies and the expansive research agenda of the Sydney-based US Studies Centre and other counterpart institutions in the United States and Australia. Public-facing research and educational institutions in both countries will be critical for government feedback, consensus-building and public engagement as the alliance becomes more intimate, mutually reliant and complex.

Finally, debate on and criticism of America should continue. The founding fathers of the country vowed to create a more perfect union – they did not claim they had one. Australian voting rules, gun control laws and relative civility in politics are all attractive to Americans frustrated with our own shortcomings. Of course, certain aspects of Australian political culture could never be transplanted in the home of the free and the land of the brave.

Ultimately, the United States is a superpower that has sustained its leadership role because Americans are not afraid of such criticism. China has undercut its own rise by bullying governments and citizens abroad who dare reproach it for its abuses of human rights, lack of transparency on COVID or military pressure on neighbours. Americans may suffer at times from a reasonableness burden (countries expect the United States to be the more reasonable of the superpowers in any clash) – but in the long run it is that reasonableness and openness to criticism that makes America the indispensable power. ■

HISTORY LESSON

The world still needs a mighty USA

Dennis Glover

What does the United States represent to Australia? An example of supercharged capitalism? A generator of our best and worst culture and ideas? A military umbrella to give us protection? A beacon of democracy? One thing most will concede is that America is the most financially and militarily powerful democracy in the world. Under President Joe Biden, as under Barack Obama, we could call it the most financially and militarily powerful *liberal* – maybe even *progressive* – democracy in the world. Some, especially on the progressive side, will disagree, arguing that America is in fact imperialist, that it only looks after itself and that its progressive, liberal-democratic values are more ideals than reality, given its broken electoral system and horrendous social inequalities – to which the only answer is that in a world of resurgent anti-liberal authoritarianism, America's failings are relative.

Today authoritarianism is on the march everywhere, becoming more aggressive, asserting the superiority of its political systems, taking a more belligerent military posture and even invading or threatening to invade neighbouring countries. Its populist support movement, united by liberal-hating ideologies with ugly echoes of the 1930s, is spreading across the world, contesting elections and sometimes winning. The choice confronting us is becoming increasingly clear. On one side, the murderous kleptocratic oligarchy of the Russian Federation and the repressive, one-party dictatorship of the People's Republic of China. On the other, America and its democratic allies, with all their political, economic and social imperfections. If forced to choose – as the Ukrainian people have already had to do – which side will it be?

For those who care about their freedoms, there is only one practical answer: America and its allies. If there is a danger to democratic countries such as Australia, it lies in an America that rejects its liberal-democratic and progressive impulses, elects a sympathiser with reactionary authoritarianism and retreats into isolationism. We may not particularly like this choice, but there it is.

What, therefore, should Australia do in relation to America? We need to put aside the "whataboutism" we usually engage in when it comes to the United States and use our diplomacy and middle-power strength to encourage America to remain liberal, democratic, progressive and engaged in the affairs of the world. Our geography suggests that discouraging illiberal and undemocratic countries from military expansion is in our direct interest. And history tells us that an America that engages in progressive alliances is the world's best hope.

History doesn't repeat – it returns better armed

Who would have guessed this is what the world would look like in 2023? That so many nations, regarded as stable democracies and governed by previously unquestioned conventions of political behaviour, would be locked in a deadly battle with authoritarian populism. Who would have expected "others" to be so demonised, opposing parties transformed into the "enemy within", truth made relative and rumblings of global conflict everywhere? Who would have expected World War II battlefields around Kharkiv to once again be rolling with tanks, Babi Yar despoiled, European cities the targets of strategic bombing, pensioners cowering in their basements in freezing midwinter darkness, children murdered by shelling and missile attacks? Who would have expected the discovery of more mass graves? And who would have thought the People's Republic of China might be seriously threatening to invade Taiwan? Historians, that's who. And if we are to save the world from destruction in this era of authoritarianism, populism and war, this potential re-run of the 1930s, history might just be our secret weapon. History doesn't so much repeat as return better armed.

Hindsight allows us to see the patterns that form – it enables us to warn the world against letting madness happen all over again. To arm decision-makers. To say, "Don't forget."

Forget what? The 1930s and '40s. Especially World War II and the mistakes that preceded it.

The disaster and horror of that conflict still have the power to shock. Six years of fighting, more if you count the Japanese invasion of Manchuria and China, Mussolini's attack on Abyssinia and the civil war in Spain. Tens of millions dead. The Holocaust. The greatest displacement of people in history. Area bombing, with dozens of cities, including medieval and renaissance treasures, razed to the ground. For Australians, the bombing of Darwin, the Changi prisoner-of-war camp, the Sandakan death march. The invention of the atomic bomb and its use on Nagasaki and Hiroshima. If historians have a key performance indicator, it is surely to stop World War II being followed by a third.

So let's try. Let's look at a crucial moment in history, a moment recognisably like today, when things could have turned out differently. If we'd been smarter. If America had not been isolationist and its allies hadn't lacked the necessary resolve. If we'd displayed greater moral leadership, earlier.

Crossing the Ebro, badly armed

There is a famous photograph of a squad of Spanish Republican soldiers wading across a knee-deep section of the river Ebro in front of the town of Miravet in late July 1938. The image makes us think of what might have been – it is a clue to everything the world got wrong in the 1930s. Understand what happened in the Spanish Civil War and, as Russian forces assault Ukraine and China flexes its muscles in Asia, you understand where our world is at today.

On 24 July 1938, the Spanish Republic's 5th and 15th Army Corps crossed the Ebro and attacked their Nationalist opponents in an attempt to demonstrate to the democratic world, which had forsaken it, that after two years of fighting, the Spanish Republic was still alive, still capable of offensive operations, a black mark on the democratic world's conscience, a black mark which might still be erased. Around the world, supporters of the Spanish Republic held their breath. Maybe, they thought, Britain, France and America would finally end their policy of non-intervention and arm the Spanish democracy as a bulwark against fascism, allowing it to hang on until the now inevitable-looking European war broke out.

At first the offensive worked, liberating hundreds of square kilometres from fascist rule. But within a week the operation was revealed as the folly it always was. The Republican forces started with a severe disadvantage. Lacking sufficient trucks, artillery, tanks and aircraft, they were at the mercy of a highly mechanised and well-armed opposition, which had been supplied with the most up-to-date transport and weaponry by Nazi Germany and Fascist Italy. On the exposed rocky plains and hills of the open battleground, the Republican armies were pounded by plentiful and modern artillery and aircraft and confronted by fresh troops rushed to the front by thousands of American trucks supplied and fuelled on generous terms of credit by Ford, General Motors, Studebaker, Du Pont, Rio Tinto Zinc and the Texas Oil

Company. Among the Nationalist forces was the German Condor Legion, which would use the battle to test the tactics and weapons Hitler would later deploy against France, Britain, the Low Countries and Russia. Stubbornly and probably unwisely, thinking their Ebro attack a gallant example to the democratic world, the Republican troops hung on until 16 November, when they retreated back across the river to their old defensive positions. Their armies were now effectively destroyed. The final Nationalist offensive then commenced, leaving massacre in its wake. On 26 January Barcelona fell, followed two months later by Madrid and Valencia. On 1 April the war was over. The terms were unconditional surrender. The round-ups and executions accelerated. The concentration camps began to fill and would remain in operation until Francisco Franco, the last of the world's 1930s fascist dictators, died in 1975. Six months after the Republic fell, World War II began.

Fascist nations acted, democratic nations did nothing

How had this happened? It's simple: fascist nations acted, democratic nations did nothing. When the Spanish generals attempted their coup on 17 July 1936 and failed to swiftly decapitate the Republic, they appealed to Hitler and Franco to come to their aid. Luftwaffe transport aircraft were provided to fly advance units of Franco's Spanish Army of Africa across the Mediterranean, German pocket battleships kept the Spanish Republican Navy from intervening, plentiful weapons and munitions were supplied, and eventually German and Italian expeditionary forces directly joined the fighting.

The Republic's best hope was to be similarly armed and supported by Britain, France, the United States and other democracies. Instead, those nations, led most forcefully by the British foreign secretary, Anthony Eden, organised a policy of "non-intervention". The United States remained staunchly isolationist. Congress had rejected membership of the League of Nations in 1919 and during the Spanish conflict passed a series of neutrality acts making it illegal for Americans to sell or transport war materials to other nations (at the same time looking the other way as American corporations supported the Spanish Nationalists). The non-intervention policy caused the French Popular Front government to cancel its early pledge of arms to the Republic by 2 August. On 12 August a formal Non-Intervention Committee was established, including Britain, France, Germany and Italy, to impose an arms blockade on Spain, with the aim of denying arms to both sides. While the blockade was policed scrupulously by the British and grudgingly obeyed by the guilt-ridden Popular Front administration of Léon Blum, which feared provoking war with Germany and Italy without British support, it was completely ignored by the Germans and Italians, who covered their generous arming of Franco's forces with blatant subterfuges, in the process forming the Rome–Berlin Axis. The British refused to acknowledge what was really happening and allowed Royal Navy officers with Nationalistic sympathies to assist the rebels.

Quoting an American envoy of the time, the historian Giles Tremlett called the Non-Intervention Committee "the most cynical and lamentably dishonest group that history has ever known".

The Republic, meanwhile, was forced to rely on enthusiastic but mostly untrained and ill-armed international volunteers, as well as on aid from Mexico and the Soviet Union, whose grudging support was provided with political conditions that eventually helped destroy the unity of the Republic. Nothing shifted the British from this position – including the well-reported massacres of thousands of Republicans in towns such as Badajoz and the razing of Guernica by the bombers of the Condor Legion. After the failure of the Ebro campaign, the British helped organise the removal of the International Brigades, hoping it would encourage the Germans and Italians to leave. The genocide and terror bombing of the world's cities had begun. As Tremlett adds: "For the first time ever, newspaper readers around the world became used to seeing photographs of dead women and children, or of homes ripped in half by bombs, spilling their innards." Supposedly good people did nothing. As George Orwell, who fought for the Republican side, put it: "The outcome of the Spanish war was settled in London, Paris, Rome, Berlin – at any rate not in Spain ... The Fascists won because they were the stronger; they had modern arms and the others hadn't."

Would the liberal-democratic nations of the world ever learn?

The British-led attempt to appease Hitler over Spain had not only failed to end the Spanish Civil War, but it also convinced the Nazi leader that the liberal democracies would allow him to continue his expansionist plans. Their surrender to him at Munich in September 1938, just as the Republican armies were being destroyed and driven back over the Ebro, confirmed it. At this point, convinced that Britain and France could not be relied upon to fight Germany, and knowing isolationist America would not intervene, Stalin turned his thoughts towards making his historic and scandalous pact with Hitler. As Franco's armies prepared for the final assaults on Valencia and Madrid, Hitler took over the weakened Czech state. In this sense, the abandonment of the Spanish Republic was another example of failed appeasement. The leading historians of the Third Reich are insistent that the failure to counter the Axis's military interventions in Spain encouraged Hitler to set his sights on Poland. As Richard Evans put it:

> The Spanish Civil War was one more example for [Hitler] of the supine pusillanimity of Britain and France, and thus an encouragement to move faster in the fulfilment of his own intentions. In this sense at least, the Spanish conflict accelerated the descent into war.

In a moral and even tactical sense, World War II had begun in Spain when the leading democratic nations failed to react to fascist regimes as they conducted a war of terror, bombing cities and civilians and carrying out mass executions under polite public relations fictions. It could all have been stopped earlier, but wasn't. Near the end of Ken Burns' 2022 documentary *The U.S. and the Holocaust*, an actor quotes Eleanor Roosevelt's summation of the tragedy of that conflict: "We let our consciences realise too late the need of standing up against something we knew was wrong. We have therefore had to avenge it, but we did nothing to prevent it." Would the liberal-democratic nations of the world ever learn?

Into Kherson – armed by democracy

Sometimes, just sometimes, we do learn.

In October 2022, the Ukrainian army broke out of its defensive positions and began its drive to recapture the city of Kherson on the banks of Dnipro River, near the Black Sea coast. It was a crucial moment in the war that had begun with a Russian invasion of Ukrainian territory eight months earlier. Situated close to Crimea, Kherson had immense strategic importance, providing a possible staging post for the recapture of that peninsula, which had been illegally annexed by Russia in 2014. But its symbolic importance was even greater. Kherson had been the only major city to fall to the Russians after their invasion of Ukraine on 24 February, its brutal and destructive siege and surrender reported live on the world's 24-hour news channels. Its loss, therefore, would signal to the world that the war had turned in Ukraine's favour and was worth supporting. On 9 November, the Russian forces announced they were abandoning the city to fall back on a new defensive line on the eastern bank of the Dnipro. On 11 November the last of their troops left. Kherson had been liberated.

Back in February 2022, Russia expected the war to be over in a matter of days, thinking it would easily take the capital, Kyiv, decapitate the country's leadership and force capitulation. The failure of the lightning war allowed the Ukrainians, inspired by their charismatic leader Volodymyr Zelensky, to regroup, dig in and inflict punishing casualties on the invading forces while pushing them back from the outskirts of Kyiv. As in Spain in 1936, a failed seizure of power had started a drawn-out war. By August, Ukraine had become strong enough to go on the offensive, recording stunning victories to the north and east of Kharkiv, liberating an estimated 74,443 square kilometres of territory.

How had the outnumbered Ukrainian forces managed to pull off such a stunning reversal? Military experts are in general agreement on the two principal causes: the Ukrainians were united and better motivated, and the liberal democracies had armed them with superior weapons.

Just before Christmas 2022, Zelensky visited Washington, eliciting from Congress promises of continuing financial and military support – most immediately the provision of Patriot anti-missile systems to counter the aerial bombardment of Ukraine's energy infrastructure and population centres – a strategy forced on the Russians by the absence of victories on the ground. The trip, which followed many virtual addresses to Western legislatures, was an acknowledgement by

Zelensky that support from the United States and its allies is the most important factor in the outcome of the war.

The extra weapons Zelensky sought on his trip were just the latest in a long list of advanced weaponry and military training made available to Ukraine by the liberal democracies. On 10 November, as Ukrainian forces were entering Kherson, the US State Department released details of the US$18.3 billion of military assistance the US had made since the start of the war, which included significant amounts of the most up-to-date anti-tank and anti-aircraft missiles, precision artillery, tanks, armoured personnel carriers, helicopters, drones, infantry weapons and training. Europe and the UK did likewise. In January 2023, the US, the UK, German and other European governments began to provide main battle tanks, armoured personnel carriers and self-propelled artillery that would enable the Ukrainians to go on the offensive in the spring of 2023.

The Ukrainians were able to pull off a tactical victory that may become … a war-winning one

This assistance has proved decisive on the battlefield and is almost certainly the major reason why, at the time of writing, Ukraine remains free. As Zelensky remarked to US Congressmen and women on 22 December 2022, thanking them for their weapons and financial support: "Your money is not charity. It's an investment in global security and democracy that we handle in the most responsible way."

The contrast with the situation facing the Spanish Republican forces in the Ebro campaign could not be more stark. Denied modern artillery and aircraft by Western democracies, including an isolationist America, in 1938, the Republican forces were effectively defeated before they crossed the river. Provided with the modern equivalents of such weapons in 2022, the Ukrainians were able to pull off a tactical victory that may in time become a strategic, war-winning one. Were Orwell alive today, he may well have written that the outcome of this war is being decided in Washington, London, Berlin and Brussels as well as Ukraine. Seldom do we get such perfect laboratory conditions to compare the results of foreign policy decisions. The conclusion from this: the statesmen of the 1930s failed to arm democracy, stop fascism and prevent the slide into global war when they had the chance – the statesmen and women of today are succeeding. In the 1930s, America was isolationist, the European democracies non-interventionist, and the world unwilling to act. Today, the opposite is true, and democracy has the upper hand as a result.

What a Ukrainian victory would mean

In the 1930s, the main arguments for opposing aid to Spain were that arming the Spanish Republicans would upset the balance of forces between the Republicans and Nationalists and prevent them from reaching a stalemate, leading to a negotiated peace faster; encourage the Axis powers to provide more arms to the Francoists; alarm the Axis powers, stoking a supercharged arms race and provoking them into starting a wider war; embroil their own countries in a war in which they have no interest – the isolationist position; and give a potential victory to communism – the argument of those who were on Hitler's side and were happy to see the Spanish Republic crushed, no matter how much blood had to be spilled.

We hear similar arguments today from those opposed to the provision of military and financial support for Ukraine: allowing Ukraine to lose will result in fewer deaths and less destruction; arming Ukraine will only encourage Putin to escalate the war; an impending defeat will make Putin desperate, leading to the potential resort to nuclear weapons; providing military support to Ukraine will preoccupy and militarily weaken the democratic West, allowing China to increase its relative strength and invade Taiwan; and prolonging the war will further drive up the living costs that are resulting from worldwide reliance on Russian fossil fuel energy.

Putin isn't the only problem today

What these arguments say, in a roundabout way, is that for the good of world peace and prosperity we should pressure Ukraine into accepting bad peace terms, cede territory, allow its children to be slaughtered and its people to be subjected to ethnic cleansing, and become a client state of Putin's Russia. Just like the peace sought in the 1930s, which Eleanor Roosevelt lamented, such a result will lead to peace without honour that will bring war with dishonour. If the isolationist arguments of then and now seem similar, it's because they have the same psychological origin: appeasement. And like appeasement, they will inevitably fail.

When the Republican armies crossed the Ebro in 1938, they thought their courage might rally the Western democracies to step in. But it was too late – they had already turned their attention elsewhere. An emboldened Hitler was demanding the dismemberment of Czechoslovakia, creating the Munich Crisis. The democracies were discovering the price of their lack of resolution over Spain. A war with Nazi Germany was unavoidable. What's more, they had given Hitler an invaluable opportunity to test and refine the tactics and weapons that would conquer Poland in 1939, western Europe in 1940 and get him to the gates of Moscow in 1941.

The lesson from Spain is straightforward. Refusing to help a democracy defend itself when threatened and attacked by a corrupt, aggressive and irrational autocracy is a mistake that serves only to embolden the aggressor, making a larger conflict much more likely. This is what "appeasement", precisely defined, means. The term is regularly misused to justify hawkish foreign policy in situations that have only passing similarity to what happened in the 1930s – the war in Vietnam and the 2003 invasion of Iraq being the most obvious examples. Ukraine, though, gives us a textbook opportunity to learn the lessons of appeasement proper. It allows us to learn from Spain.

And just as Franco wasn't the only problem in the 1930s, Putin isn't the only problem today. In the same way that arming the Spanish

Republic would have helped defeat Franco while sending a clear message of democratic resolution to Hitler, defeating Putin in Ukraine will send a clear message of democratic resolution to China, which is today's potential destabilising force, pushing for revision of its territorial boundaries. If history is any guide, strength shown in Ukraine may encourage China to see that aggressive posturing won't allow it to get it what it wants in Taiwan, and maybe elsewhere, without a fight. In this way it may encourage China to seek more peaceful and evolutionary processes to achieve its foreign policy aims. By demonstrating their unity and the obvious capability of their weapons systems in Ukraine, liberal-democratic countries have given China powerful reasons to pause in its upping of the ante in the Asia-Pacific region. As Timothy Garton Ash has put it, should Russia win in Ukraine, "Putin would then have demonstrated to Xi Jinping, and other dictators around the world, that armed aggression and nuclear blackmail can pay off handsomely. Next stop, Taiwan."

Simple morality and historical literacy demand we act

The role for Australia

Australia has played its part in helping the Ukrainians in their struggle for survival. Our military and humanitarian assistance has been strong and consistent with our military capacity, including the provision of armoured troop carriers, drones, ammunition and infantry training.

Given the ongoing missile bombardment of Ukrainian cities – with their obvious parallels with the bombing of Guernica and of European cities afterwards – simple morality and historical literacy demand we act. So does self-interest.

As a small to middle power, our direct contribution won't make a decisive difference. Our most important contribution must therefore be diplomatic and moral – by doing everything we can to keep America, Europe and other democracies in the fight to defend freedoms which the authoritarians and populists of the world increasingly hold in contempt. In the face of Chinese muscle flexing over Taiwan, any American or European drift towards isolationism would be a disaster. Anything that encourages China to see the logic of adhering to international law would be a huge bonus, making Australia more secure.

This may be difficult for many progressives, reared on reflexive and at times perfectly justified anti-American feeling, to accept. But history shows that encouraging America and its NATO allies to support and arm Ukraine is the best way to prevent the further rise of anti-democratic populism and prevent the world from repeating something akin to World War II. Australia must do all in its power to be part of the coalition that prevents the war in Ukraine from becoming a re-run of the Spanish Civil War and a precursor to something far worse. The combined determination of countries such as the United States, its NATO allies, Japan, South Korea, Australia and others to defend liberal democracy whenever it is threatened will make populists and authoritarians recognise they can never win without paying a hefty price. As the famous Spanish Republican poster showing children killed by fascist bombing stated: “If we tolerate this, our children could be next.” ■

THE FIX *Solving Australia's foreign affairs challenges*

Andrew Carr on How to Involve the States in Foreign Policymaking

"What is needed is a new framework that embraces and strengthens the ability of the rest of Australia – beyond Canberra – to wisely and safely engage internationally."

THE PROBLEM: In mid-2020, as the pandemic raged, the Morrison government decided Australia had too many unknown entanglements with the world. Australia's state and territory governments were a particular concern, boasting nearly 100 overseas offices in more than a dozen countries, and thousands of agreements on issues of trade, the environment, access for business and local investment. These links, once celebrated in the age of globalisation, were now viewed darkly, as exemplified by Victoria's participation in China's Belt and Road Initiative.

The more involvement in global networks, so the logic went, the more avenues for Australians to be coerced by foreign governments. Watch TikTok videos and your data will be visible to spies in Beijing. Send money overseas via SWIFT and Washington can track your payments, or even disconnect countries from the network, as it did to Russia in 2022. In such a world, a bumbling state government, blithely seeking to encourage local industry, could soon find itself beholden to blackmail or laden with debt.

By the end of 2020, the *Australia's Foreign Relations Act* was passed, giving the foreign minister a veto over all agreements with foreign countries by state and territory governments (and universities). The aim, the prime minister said, was "to ensure that Australia, not just at a federal level, but across all of our governments, speak with one voice".

However, the problem here, described by scholars as "weaponised interdependence", is not overcome by unity. Research has shown that countries which tightly control their economies are just as much at risk as open market economies. And, counterintuitively, larger economies can be more exposed than smaller ones, since they have more links and more reasons for others to want to influence them.

Since it's impossible to avoid participating in global commerce and technology networks, the only way to reduce or avoid coercion is to understand how these networks are structured, and to show vigilance in how they might be exploited. The 2020 legislation does not solve this problem. It potentially makes it worse by insisting on a "minister knows best" approach. What is needed is a new framework that embraces and strengthens the ability of the rest of Australia – beyond Canberra – to wisely and safely engage internationally. Done right, such an approach could also unlock significant new resources for Australian diplomacy.

THE PROPOSAL: The federal government should pursue a "Team of States" model, building a foreign policy apparatus of Australia's non-central governments (NCGs) – states, territories, and city and local councils – to engage with the world. A policy that is confident in its pursuit of Australian interests, cooperative in spirit and conscious of the risks of a darkening international environment. The aim should be to decentralise diplomatic knowledge and skills.

First, the Australian government should make a specific investment in DFAT. Perhaps start small by expanding the state and territory offices of the Trade and Investment Strategy Branch, and, in time, create a dedicated office to support, train and share information with NCG foreign advisory offices. The size, expertise and practices of these offices vary widely. A 2019 review of Western Australia's overseas presence found "substantially different practices" across offices, with problems of accountability, process, coordination and information sharing. Other states face similar concerns.

Second, the Australian government needs to establish a more open, decentralised foreign policy culture. The R.G. Casey building cannot be the funnel through which Australia speaks to the world. Not even the federal government operates that way, with most major departments already having a significant overseas presence. Similar trust and cooperation should be expanded to Australia's NCGs. They need to know what other parts of Australia are doing, and they need access to many of the intelligence sources that would help them understand the region. Imagine a world where Victorian officials had access to the same risks and opportunities analysis of the Belt and Road scheme as Canberra had from the very beginning, enabling a common federal–state position to emerge. Or, as Western Australia's defence industry minister, Paul Papalia, recently requested, where WA police, who keep that state's long coastline secure, are allowed to see what the ADF's maritime patrols see.

In return, Australian NCGs will need to make their own commitments. They need to invest in and sustain their international presence. States first sent representatives overseas in 1894, with James McInnes Sinclair's trade mission to the United States, Canada and Argentina, but attention has waxed and waned with economic cycles and the proclivities of specific premiers and chief ministers. At times, the competition between NCGs has seen a "beggar thy neighbour" attitude in the pursuit of overseas contracts, to the cost of national interests.

Finally, there are times when the federal government will need to have the last say, and this will have to be accepted, not griped about to overseas leaders, as has sometimes occurred. To help regain trust, the *Foreign Relations Act* should be significantly revised. The requirement in Part 2 of the act for ministerial approval before negotiations can even begin should be removed. So too the test in Parts 3 and 4 that "inconsistency" with national policy is sufficient for a veto. Instead, only the most pressing security concerns should be able to justify a federal override.

WHY IT WILL WORK: Some readers may wonder if this model is too naive for the hard world of foreign relations. Yet those tasked with lethal foreign relations – our armed forces – have shown decentralised, transparent models are not only possible but *necessary* in complex and networked environments. Under notions of "Mission Command", responsibility and information are pushed down to those on the ground, helping them lead the organisation from the frontlines. As the former US Special Forces commander Stanley McChrystal has explained, in a complex world "adaptability, not efficiency, must become our central competency".

The diverse skill sets, identities and relationships which state governments and Australian civil society have are incredibly valuable. We need that diversity if we are to understand, adapt and be resilient in a difficult world. For instance, why not push the locus of Australia's relationship with the South Pacific into Queensland. Our people up north – especially the Torres Strait Islanders – share the same climate and are the first to help in the face of common environmental disasters. Likewise, the Northern Territory has special links with Timor-Leste, and Western Australia increasingly is, and should be, proud to be Australia's gateway to India. Canberra of course will have a crucial role in these relationships, but under a Team of States model it won't always have to be the loudest voice. Such a framework fits neatly with very welcome recent moves to strengthen First Nations voices in Australian foreign policy.

While many have urged the Albanese government to rebuild DFAT after two decades of damage – and it should – there is an existing 130-year-old set of relationships between Australia and the world that is underappreciated, if not cowed, thanks to the 2020 legislation. Shifting to a Team of States approach could develop a genuinely twenty-first-century vision of Australian foreign policy. One which recognises that in a networked, complex world, the heart and wisdom of our foreign policy is not found in legislated edicts but in the daily acts of all Australians.

THE RESPONSE: The office of the Minister for Foreign Affairs declined to respond. ■

Reviews

Helpem Fren: Australia and the Regional Assistance Mission to Solomon Islands
Michael Wesley
Melbourne University Press

In *Helpem Fren: Australia and the Regional Assistance Mission to Solomon Islands*, Michael Wesley rightly describes RAMSI – as the Australian-led intervention came to be known – as one of Australia's "most audacious and complex foreign policy undertakings". Yet the mission was "quietly forgotten" by most Australians, long before its fourteen-year deployment came to an end in 2017.

The early chapters – elegantly titled *Lineages, Descent and Resolve* – are the strongest and go some way towards explaining this conundrum. Wesley provides concise yet insightful accounts of the drivers – in Australia and Solomon Islands – that two decades ago culminated in Canberra boldly abandoning its long-held bipartisan orthodoxy of hands-off engagement with the Pacific. Instead, the Howard government actively lobbied Australia's island neighbours to join it in forming, if not funding, a regional intervention force to be deployed to what was by then, a much-troubled Solomon Islands.

Wesley details the antecedents of white Australia's colonial insecurities that led it to look to the Pacific island countries with, as he puts it, "a combination of anxiety and arrogance." He unearths bizarre aspirations, such as the one advocated in 1872 requiring aggressive British colonisation of the Pacific isles in order to create an "Anglo-Saxon Sea" stretching from the shores of California to Queensland.

He also highlights the pivotal role of the Australian colonies in agitating Britain to annex – reluctantly – the linguistically and culturally disparate Solomons archipelago into a single entity under British rule in 1893. This effectively laid the foundation, where none really existed, for the creation of the "independent" nation of Solomon Islands in 1978. Although Wesley acknowledges that this was a construct of "external convenience" more than "internal aspirations", he is silent on the grand irony that within a quarter of a century Australia felt the need to lead and largely pay for a mission to "rebuild" this so-called state.

Helpem Fren's detailed account of the Howard government's volte-face, executed in ninety-three days, along with a deftly interwoven account of the precision of the planning and clockwork "shock and awe" deployment of a fully-fledged regional mission on 24 July 2003 to the Solomons, are the book's most compelling chapters. Unfortunately, it is in the pages that follow this depiction of the mission's early glory days – when Solomon Islanders' overwhelming support for RAMSI saw it exceed its own expectations in getting the guns off the street, hosing down the tensions, and stopping the financial bleeding – that the book, like the mission, appears to lose its way.

To his credit, Wesley is upfront about the limits of the book, declaring in his preface that he is attempting a history of RAMSI from an *Australian* perspective (reviewer's emphasis) based on the materials he was able to access. While quick to add that this approach should not be misconstrued as an attempt to paint RAMSI as an "Australian-only" operation, this caveat is not enough to exonerate all of the book's shortcomings.

Helpem Fren both reflects and rewards DFAT for its decision to open its "books" to the author – including thousands of yet unclassified diplomatic cables generated over the life of the mission – but ultimately suffers as a result. At times, it is hard to shake off the impression that you are reading an official history of Australia's role in the intervention, particularly during the long stretches of eye-glazing detail on the vicissitudes of the mission's reform efforts in Solomon Islands. Whether discussing the Australian Federal Police's (AFP) frequently clunky attempts to simultaneously work with, purge and rebuild the rightly maligned Royal Solomon Islands Police Force (RSIPF), or AusAID's overblown Machinery of Government program, which more than once threatened to balloon into a mission of its own, the book regularly loses the reader in a morass of detail. In the chapters covering the challenges facing RAMSI's efforts to rebuild a "failing" state, the author appears at times to have got a little lost in the weeds (read cables). It's an approach that not only sees *Helpem Fren* lose the easy narrative pace of its opening chapters but limits the reader's ability to absorb the author's careful analysis of the elements – within the Solomons body politic and the mission's own design – that ultimately led to RAMSI's failure to bring about the shifts so desired in and for Solomon Islands, despite a $2.6 billion bill for Australia's contribution alone.

Wesley clearly went to some effort to garner a greater understanding of Solomon Islands beyond what was available to him from the cables authored by Australian diplomats and development experts. Making several trips to the country during the six years he worked on the book, he interviewed the prime minister who invited RAMSI in, Sir Allan Kemakeza, and the prime minister who in 2006 wanted to kick RAMSI out, Manasseh Sogavare, the country's current PM. However, the author's conclusions at times reflect an uneven understanding of some aspects of what, it must be conceded, is, culturally and politically, a complex country.

Helpem Fren's discussion of RAMSI's exploration of community policing is a case in point. The initiative had considerable initial support from some of the more culturally insightful leaders within RAMSI's Participating Police Force (PPF), as well as a groundswell of support from within the RSIPF, particularly provincial police commanders charged with policing vast stretches of the nation's islands and ocean with very limited resources, *and* a highly successful pilot – yet the AFP who staffed the leadership of the PPF ultimately put the kibosh on it. The failure to recognise community policing as likely the most cost effective and culturally appropriate solution to the country's policing challenges remains one of RAMSI's greatest negative legacies. Wesley's perfunctory dismissal of this in one paragraph as being due to "funding limitations" is a disappointing example of the pitfalls of such heavy reliance on the Australian perspective.

More problematic is a section in the book's final chapter, *Drawdown*, in which Wesley resorts to the trope of young black men as troublemakers. Attempting to paint a picture of the nation as the mission departs in 2017, he dismisses the country's ill-served youth as "knots of unemployed, bored young men … hanging around …looking for trouble" when, in reality, the majority are just looking for something to do. Despite declining access to their traditional cultures, and the state's continuing failure to provide adequate education or economic opportunities, the vast majority of Solomon Islands youth – thus far – manage to pass their days with the help of two Melanesian favourites – betel nut and *tok stori* – telling stories. If it was trouble they were after, as Wesley suggests, Solomon Islanders would not enjoy the relative peace of everyday life that they currently cherish between events such as Honiara's politically inspired riots of 2021. Although a distressing decline in standards of governance, economic stresses, growing poverty and rapid urbanisation suggest this can't last, the past two decades of largely harmonious coexistence in this post-conflict society may prove to have been, as Wesley points out, the most enduring legacy of RAMSI's partnership with Solomon Islanders.

The book's appropriately fulsome acknowledgement that RAMSI would "not have been possible without the extraordinary contributions from other Pacific countries, and talented people from across the region, not the least Solomon Islands" does not make up for the cursory references to the contributions of the other fourteen participating countries, including New Zealand. Instead, *Helpem Fren* lacks a sense of the Pacific verve and tick that was in many ways the lifeblood of the mission and a big part of what made RAMSI so uniquely successful in its relationship with the majority of Solomon Islanders.

A succession of impressive (and a few not so impressive) New Zealand deputy special coordinators is not mentioned. These experienced diplomats would for periods act as head of mission; the best of whom provided a crucial counterbalance to the occasional gung-ho idea, particularly those espoused by some of the less capable PPF commanders, who were dispatched by the AFP without seeming regard for the emotional intelligence or cross-cultural skills required. Although Wesley deals with the Pacific Island Forum's oversight of RAMSI in considerable detail, he dwells only briefly on the decision, in the first year to create the role of an assistant special coordinator so that a senior Pacific Islander could be slotted into the RAMSI executive. This repaired an oversight that had occurred at the mission's inception which initially left its leadership without Pacific representation and so without capacity to be more alive to cultural and community issues that may not be so obvious to the Australians and New Zealanders.

The lack of any sustained attempt to capture the reality on the ground of the Pacific nature of the mission means *Helpem Fren* misses the significance of contributions such as that of the late Mataiasi Lomaloma, known universally and affectionately as Masi. An experienced UN peacekeeper and senior Fijian public servant, Lomaloma was seconded into the role of assistant special coordinator in 2005. Serving to the mission's end in 2017, he became RAMSI's longest serving leader, providing not only an extraordinary repository of corporate memory but a deep well of Pacific wisdom and cultural understanding upon which the RAMSI leadership was only too grateful to draw in some of the mission's darkest moments. This includes two separate incidents that resulted in the deaths of Solomon Islanders at the hands of RAMSI personnel. It's unclear why Wesley chose not to examine these, both of which had the potential to put at risk RAMSI's continued presence in the country. If he had, there would have been much to learn from an examination of the RAMSI executive's actions in the wake of these deaths, about the quality of the mission's leadership at the time but also the deep respect with which they treated their partnership with the Solomon Islands government and people.

Another significant anomaly is Wesley's use of the term "murder" to refer to the untimely death in 2002 of the New Zealand deputy high commissioner, Bridget Nichols. She was fatally wounded in the lung with her own fruit knife while carrying boxes down an uneven garden path at her residence shortly after she arrived in country. Investigations undertaken by a taskforce of New Zealand, Australian and Solomon Islands police – as well as by the Solomon Islands equivalent of a coroner's inquiry, conducted by the country's Chief Magistrate – found no evidence that Nichols' death was due to foul play. The New Zealand government publicly accepted these findings, so it's unclear why the author has not.

Although he refers to it more than once, Wesley also understates the significance of Talking Truth, the popular talkback program broadcast nationally on Solomon Islands Broadcasting Corporation, and inexplicably fails to acknowledge that it was a creation of RAMSI. The program was central to the success of the mission's earliest strategic communications, bringing the Solomon Islands and RAMSI leadership right into the homes and villages of Solomon Islanders. This did much to allay public concerns about the intervention and to pre-empt or address misinformation in the tense days leading up to RAMSI's deployment and for much of the early life of the mission, reflecting RAMSI's early and genuine commitment to transparency. The brainchild of Australian communications specialist Kate Graham and expertly hosted by the fluent and fearless Solomon Islands journalist Dorothy Wickham, *Talking Truth* instantly gave a sense of being seen, heard and informed to a nation starved of information about the goings on in their own country. Accompanying RAMSI's first provincial outreaches, where communities were given an open invitation to ask the mission's leaders questions live-on-air, the program also played to the strengths of RAMSI's first special coordinator, Nick Warner, and his AFP sidekick, the PPF's inaugural commander, Ben McDevitt, who, despite their lack of Solomon Islands pidgin, managed to read – and win over – a room or a village time and again.

For all this, *Helpem Fren* remains a highly valuable contribution due to the considerable amount of knowledge it adds to the public record about this bold, if little-recognised, mission and its deployment to one of Australia's least understood neighbours. The author's expertise in the art of state building provides welcome insights throughout. Most pertinent of these is the observation that Canberra's initial, sudden, and seemingly unbounding enthusiasm for rebuilding a failed state reflected a wider zeitgeist among Western nations about the benefits – forget the burden – of imposing Western neoliberal institutions on countries that were barely functioning.

Conversely, in the face of the subsequent ignoble fate of state-building exercises in places such as Iraq and Afghanistan, the gradual loss of such conviction internationally over the life of RAMSI's mission fed directly into Canberra's pragmatic unwinding of the mission. In 2011 and 2012, the preconditions for the mission's withdrawal – the achievement of defined and sustainable economic, governance and security reforms – were replaced by funding limits and deadlines. This signified the real end of the original multifaceted RAMSI. The military contingent withdrew in 2013 and the civilian reform program transitioned to Australia and New Zealand's bilateral development programs, effectively reducing the mission to a civilian-led police capacity-building exercise under the RAMSI brand for its final four years.

It was the ultimate concession of defeat in terms of RAMSI's original state-rebuilding aspirations. Especially as these original aspirations were not only those of Australia, New Zealand and the participating Pacific nations, but were also shared by so many ordinary Solomon Islanders, who wholeheartedly embraced RAMSI's oft articulated vision to partner them in building "a peaceful, stable and prosperous nation".

Ultimately *Helpem Fren* upholds Wesley's contention in its opening pages that "Australia's engagement with the Pacific is a story of passions outstripping actions, of ambitions outstripping abilities" – a lesson re-learnt from RAMSI that remains pertinent to this day.

Mary-Louise O'Callaghan

From Development to Democracy: The Transformations of Modern Asia
Dan Slater and Joseph Wong
Princeton University Press

What's to become of democracy? Backsliding, illiberal turns and inequality across the West have sparked growing anxiety that the centre is not holding. Just 6 per cent of young people in the UK believe their votes shape policy decisions, while half of their American cousins believe their country is "in trouble" or a "failed democracy". In South-East Asia, the democracy scorecard is spottier. As elections loom across the region, backsliding is more immediately obvious but strong people-led movements are evidence of a popular trust in democracy.

In February 2024, Indonesia will hold an enormous one-day election. Campaigning is well underway, as candidates for offices from president down to local heads vie for the hundreds of millions of votes on offer. The promise of President Joko Widodo, barred by the constitution from running for a third term, has faded since his genuinely exciting 2014 win. No likely candidates will be able to replicate his first campaign, which reinvigorated hopes for the region's most vibrant democracy.

In Malaysia, where December's general election saw the rise of Anwar Ibrahim to the top job after a long career including stints in prison, a resurgent hardline Islamic conservative wing is threatening to destabilise the fragile political system. Voters in Thailand will go to the polls in May for an election drawn along old lines – military-aligned candidates against the emergent second generation of the Thaksin Shinawatra–backed political clan – and with a constitution that all but guarantees a military dominated government.

Cambodia's prime minister Hun Sen is already on a war footing ahead of a vote there in July this year, with the forced shuttering of one of the country's few remaining independent media outlets, Voice of Democracy, and fresh attacks on opposition party Candlelight. The military junta that seized power in Myanmar in February 2021 and has unleashed hell on the country promises some form of "elections" this year, but they will not be fair or free and will almost certainly be boycotted by the remarkable Civil Disobedience Movement. Aung San Suu Kyi's National League for Democracy and other allied parties have been dissolved following the introduction of an electoral registration law.

Democracy isn't a strictly Western phenomenon, political scientists Joseph Wong and Dan Slater stress early on in *From Development to Democracy*. The pair home in on developmental Asia, a grouping of twelve states based less on geography and more on policy priorities: primarily, each has an export-led economy with heavy state-sponsored industrialisation but also private companies that are vital to development.

This definition leads to a grab bag of nations that at first appears jarring. China, certainly no democracy, receives as much of a look-in as Taiwan, Japan and South Korea – three of Asia-Pacific's most stable democracies, though they are not without their challenges.

Wong and Slater's framework for understanding how democracy has flourished in some former authoritarian states and floundered in others challenges much of the political orthodoxy. In one of the book's strongest chapters, focusing on what the pair call "developmental Britannia" – former British colonies Hong Kong, Singapore and Malaysia – they note that the strong judicial and financial institutions left by the British after independence (or the handover, in Hong Kong's case) were built upon to create some of Asia's most noted economic "miracles".

Common wisdom suggests that more development leads to more democratic concessions. Yet, as Wong and Slater write: "There is no version of modernisation theory that can make sense of Singapore's endurance as an authoritarian regime governing a society with a per capita income reaching USD$60,000." Still, they note, extreme cost-of-living pressures and a widening income inequality gap is leading to questions from Singaporean voters. Why continue voting for the same old if the same old is making chicken rice at the hawker more expensive and home ownership a pipe dream?

For Singapore's "one-party dominant state", as People's Action Party (PAP) cadres delicately put it, this inequality is a serious challenge to primacy. The PAP is consistently trending downwards in general elections – a key indicator, in Wong and Slater's framework, that a regime may be approaching the "bittersweet spot" in which further concessions must be made for elites to retain power. What such concessions may look like is not in Wong and Slater's remit, but it's an intriguing question for Singaporean voters and watchers.

Electoral signals are happily ignored by the ruling elite of Thailand. Infamously home to record-setting coups – thirteen since the fall of absolute monarchy in the 1930s, the most of any country in modern history – and heavy-handed constitution rewrites, Thailand's imminent elections are all but certain to see opposition parties, led by the Thaksin Shinawatra–founded Pheu Thai Party, dominate the popular vote but not take government.

In Slater and Wong's analysis, Thailand sits alongside Indonesia and Myanmar in the "developmental militarist" cluster of regimes that have moved towards – and, in Thailand and Myanmar's cases, subsequently reversed away from – democracy. Indonesia, they argue, succeeded where Thailand failed largely thanks to the Golkar Party, the country's oldest and New Order–backed party. Golkar, unlike the two opposition parties, was permitted and encouraged to establish regional bases across the archipelago, giving it an enormous boost through name recognition.

Though Golkar's star is on the wane now, this initial dominance gave the elite an off-ramp into electoral democracy after the fall of the Suharto regime in 1998. Many watchers in the early days of the *Reformasi* period expected a return to military rule in some form, but, Wong and Slater write, Golkar provided the vehicle to establish political legitimacy, helped along by a pre-1998 opposition splintered by the demands of electoral politics.

This is not the case in Bangkok, where conservatives' "continued dependence on the monarchy rather than a cohesive conservative political party" adds to electoral instability. A youth and rural-led pro-democracy movement resurged in 2019 and 2020, before being briefly defanged during the pandemic, and the stakes for a peaceful return to democracy appear higher again.

I deeply appreciate Wong and Slater's emphasis on the impact of the Cold War–era annihilation of leftist leaders and their supporters across the region by domestic conservative forces and their Cold War–weary Western backers, as well as on the influence of Japan during the decades in which China was preoccupied with violent upheaval at home. Both historical aspects appear forgotten in contemporary literature and analysis, which focuses on China's current influence on the region and the dominance of strongman conservative leadership.

Similarly, Wong and Slater go to great lengths to elevate the significance of the Asian Financial Crisis of 1997 and 1998 for change in Indonesia, Thailand, Taiwan and Malaysia. The crisis is given its due as a multigenerational region-defining phenomenon that shifted focus away from the economic juggernaut reputations of the '90s to political cataclysm, similar to what we see in the West with the 2008 Global Financial Crisis. As part of the millennial cohort of analysts focusing on the region with no personal memory of that time – perhaps *because* of that lack of first-hand experience – I found the analysis of its lasting impact was one of the great strengths of this comprehensive, scholarly look at the region.

Early on, Wong and Slater note the people power movement that ousted Ferdinand Marcos in the Philippines is not part of the remit of this work. This is, they write, because the Philippines' economic story differs from those states included. The shuttering of Manila's major thoroughfare in 1986 – as nuns stood alongside students and military officials demanding democracy – is an iconic snapshot of Asian democratic movements, but it is an outlier. The road from authoritarian rule to democracy in Asia is long and far less photogenic.

Erin Cook

Digital Transnationalism: Chinese-Language Media in Australia
Wanning Sun and Haiqing Yu
Brill

Digital media is often associated with censorship and authoritarianism in the Chinese context, but Wanning Sun and Haiqing Yu's *Digital Transnationalism: Chinese-Language Media in Australia* challenges this dominant view. The authors look at the role of Chinese-language digital media, especially WeChat, in Australian–Chinese diaspora communities and argue that such platforms cannot be simplistically viewed as being controlled by the Chinese Communist Party (CCP) alone. Instead, the book recognises the agency of individuals who resist and criticise censorship and political oppression, and sheds light on the transnational experience of first-generation migrants from the People's Republic of China.

This book presents a thorough analysis of the Chinese-language digital media landscape in Australia, with a specific emphasis on WeChat subscription accounts (WSAs) and "self-media" (*zimeiti*, which refers to a wide range of user-generated and non-official accounts on social media platforms), in order to explore how digital media has become crucial for staying connected with family and friends, engaging in Australian ways of life, accessing information, innovating business models and making money. However, the authors also show the challenges that come with these practices, such as political censorship, government surveillance and the limitations of the platform itself. While the book highlights concern about some Australia-based Chinese media outlets' close connections with the Overseas Chinese Affairs Office and by implication with the United Front Work Department of the CCP Central Committee, it acknowledges that there are differing views on the extent of Chinese influence on Chinese-language media in Australia.

The research, based on surveys and in-depth interviews, makes it clear that Chinese-language digital media cater to the needs of first-generation migrants in articulating an identity of "in-betweenness" and in coping with the daily challenges they face and the unique nature of Australia–China relations. While new Chinese migrants may be interested in adopting Australian values such as freedom and democracy, it's challenging due to pressure from their homeland's heavy censorship and the difficulties of adjusting to a new cultural environment. Through platforms such as WeChat, *Sing Tao Daily* and self-media accounts, Chinese-language digital media act as cultural intermediaries and opinion leaders, facilitating a sense of belonging and confidence among Chinese migrants in Australia. Nevertheless, while Chinese-language digital media may foster bonding within the first-generation migrant community, it may not be as effective in bridging the gap with other Mandarin-speaking communities from South-East Asia, Hong Kong and Taiwan or with mainstream society. Other scholars have noted that the absence of data protection for Chinese-language digital media users poses a significant challenge, and there are concerns about the CCP monitoring users. These issues raise questions about the extent to which WeChat can facilitate broader civic engagement and participation. WeChat accounts that are based in Australia, for instance, can be subject to censorship or control by the Chinese government if they operate in China or have a significant Chinese audience. Digital media were initially heralded as a force for greater democratisation and cosmopolitanism but have also been associated with division and exclusion.

This book uses the concept of "flexible citizenship" to re-examine the identity politics of first-generation Chinese immigrants in Australia. To retain flexibility and access benefits, some Chinese migrants choose to remain permanent residents instead of obtaining citizenship, while others opt for one spouse to become an Australian citizen while the other retains Chinese citizenship. Despite their enthusiasm for such flexible citizenship, Mandarin-speaking migrants face challenges such as China's rise and geopolitical dynamics, which can lead to difficulties in escaping narrow conceptions of Chinese or Australian identity.

The COVID-19 pandemic provides a prism for exploring the myriad complex, and often paradoxical, citizenship strategies of PRC migrants in Australia. The authors examine how transnational spaces, such as WeChat, allow users to articulate a feeling of being "stuck in the middle" against the backdrop of escalating tensions in the Australia–China relationship. While WeChat provides a valuable forum for political expression, other outlets and strategies are used by Chinese migrants to navigate their citizenship in Australia. Therefore, it may be necessary to consider non-Chinese-language digital media platforms, such as Facebook and Twitter, which are also used by first-generation Mandarin speakers in Australia.

The conclusion of the book, "Chinese Media and Soft Power in Australia", highlights the need for a nuanced understanding of Chinese-language media in Australia, particularly in relation to censorship, independence and influence. The authors call into question the concept of influence, which assumes that media messages are "directly injected" into the brains of passive audiences. Instead, the authors argue that pro-China content or content that abstains from criticising China may have more to do with commercialisation of rhetorical nationalism and compliance with the platform's censorship regime and regulatory framework. Sun and Yu conclude that the Australian government should invest in Australia's Chinese-language media to encourage content that is critical, impartial and addresses local concerns. However, they caution against funding this sector as a foreign policy initiative, as it is essential for Chinese-language media to maintain their independence and to avoid being associated with public diplomacy agendas.

Digital Transnationalism provides valuable insights into the role of digital media in the everyday practices of Chinese immigrants, but it falls short in addressing the fact that social media use is highly gendered – women rely heavily on digital media as a tool for social interaction and information seeking, including in relation to sensitive issues such as domestic violence. Therefore, it is imperative that future research delves deeper into gender differences in digital media use among Chinese immigrants, in order to inform the development of policies and practices that are tailored to meet the needs of the Chinese diaspora in Australia.

Nevertheless, the book provides an insightful examination of the emergence of a new transnational Chinese subjectivity. The authors' research reveals that the lack of critical discourse on China in Chinese-language digital media does not necessarily stem from a desire to promote China's interests, but rather from commercial imperatives as media outlets cater to the emotional, economic and cultural needs of their target audience. The book is replete with fascinating examples and anecdotes that illustrate how first-generation Chinese migrants have leveraged digital media over the past two decades to expand their "citizen-making practices". This new realm of Chinese social participation in Australia represents a significant development, and Sun and Yu have provided a timely and comprehensive analysis of it.

Mei-fen Kuo

Correspondence

"Sea of Many Flags" by Rory Medcalf

Zhou Fangyin

In "Sea of Many Flags" (Australian Foreign Affairs 17), Rory Medcalf argues that China has strategic intentions for the Pacific islands, and its expanding influence would directly jeopardise Australian interests, so Australia should join with other countries to build the resilience of the Pacific against China's control. The essay argues that China is attempting to dominate the Pacific region as part of its challenge to the United States globally.

It makes sense for China, Australia, New Zealand, Japan, the United States and European countries to develop relations with Pacific island countries. The essay acknowledges that China's involvement in Pacific affairs is legitimate, and excluding China is not what most of the region's governments and peoples want. However, Medcalf believes China's presence in the Pacific islands has a set goal: to control them. Thus, he establishes a basis for criticising China's rising influence. Yet there is no solid evidence that China wants to control the islands. No official Chinese document shows such an intention, much less a plan to do so. It is not clear why China would want to control Pacific island countries or what this would accomplish.

Although China is the second-largest economy in the world, it does not control any other country. China adheres to the foreign policy principle of "non-interference in internal affairs" and does not believe that controlling other countries is feasible or desirable. The essay acknowledges that there is no evidence that China has a grand strategy for the Pacific. In fact, the United States and Australia have from time to time requested island countries take sides by demonstrating anti-China attitudes. However, China will not pressure Pacific island countries to take sides between it and the US. The essay assumes that Australia needs to decide who should and should not play an important role in the Pacific, which itself reflects Australia's intention to control the region's affairs.

Medcalf takes US special influence in Micronesia for granted and says that the America "has tended to leave the development and security of Melanesia to Australia", which is not only an implicit acknowledgement that the US has control over Pacific affairs, but also that the US has transferred part of its control to Australia. In addition, France has substantial naval forces across the region and administers the Pacific territories of New Caledonia, but Medcalf has no intention of criticising France, as it is an important partner for Australia to work with to curb China's influence. There is clearly inconsistency here.

Similar double standards exist elsewhere. For example, the essay claims that China's loans have created debt problems in the Pacific island countries, while at the same time praising Japanese and Asian Development Bank loans for promoting sustainable fisheries. Medcalf sees India's cooperation with island countries as a big developing country helping smaller ones, while China's cooperation is seen as a reflection of a rising power's ambition. Simply put, it is not the action itself that is blamed, but rather who takes that action.

Pacific island countries, as sovereign international actors, have the right to determine their own internal and foreign affairs. They have enough political wisdom and international discernment to know what is in their national interests and do not need other countries to make decisions for them, whether that country is China, the United States or Australia.

Pacific island countries are concerned about climate change, environmental protection, sustainable development, improving infrastructure, enhancing education and health service capacity. They generally do not want to be involved in complex great-power competition, and do not want other countries to dictate and run their affairs. If Australia wishes to make itself more popular with the islands, it needs to do more than target China. It needs to respect the Pacific islands, listen to them, treat them on a more equal footing and cooperate with them in ways that are beneficial to them.

I believe China has been very open about how it tries to develop partnerships in the region. If China's behaviour is not welcomed by the island countries, they will not be forced to accept it. If China's cooperation brings significant benefits to the islands, enhances their capacity for independent development and is welcomed by their governments and people, then Australia's efforts to crowd out China's influence by playing up the Chinese threat will hardly be successful.

Zhou Fangyin is a professor at the School of International Relations, Guangdong University of Foreign Studies.

Bernard Yegiora

Rory Medcalf sees China as a growing risk and suggests that Australia should lead a multinational effort to try to counter China's influence in the Pacific region. He names a list of countries which should be part of the multinational team. He's correct in saying that Australia has very good knowledge of all the countries in the Pacific region and should take the leadership role. But, if such a team develops, I do not believe it would be in Papua New Guinea's interests to join.

Anthony Albanese was given a rare opportunity to speak in PNG's Parliament House earlier this year, where he expressed Australia's view of PNG as an equal in their relationship. Yet, to treat PNG as an equal, Australia must respect PNG's view of China as an alternative development partner, tolerate PNG's "open relationship" status and encourage more trade and investment in the PNG market.

In 1975, during the Cold War era, Michael Somare, PNG's first prime minister, came up with the foreign policy approach of "friends to all, enemies to none". He wanted to diversify the country's relations to benefit economically from different nations regardless of their ideological orientation. He commissioned a policy review in 1979, which led to the 1982 "Active and Selective Engagement" foreign policy white paper written by the government of Julius Chan. The white paper maintained the approach of working with different countries, including Australia and China, to help in PNG's development.

Fast forward to 2018, when the decision by then prime minister Peter O'Neill to sign up to the Belt and Road Initiative reinforced the perspective that China is an alternative development partner. Labelled as pro-Chinese by Australian National University emeritus fellow Ron May, O'Neill's effort to consolidate and extend PNG's relations with China resonated with his foreign policy approach of "connecting for peace and prosperity in a changing world".

In 2021, as reported in *The National*, the former defence force commander Gilbert Toropo gave a public speech about the Australian-funded rehabilitation of the naval base at Lombrum and said that China's growing presence was a challenge to PNG's security. Australian media published his speech but he was told by Prime Minister James Marape to correct his statement. Marape has since mentioned repeatedly that he sees China as an important alternative development partner.

PNG has an "open relationship" with all countries and is not a strong ally of any particular nation on Medcalf's list. PNG talked with Australia about the Pacific Labour Mobility program, it is working with the EU on the ongoing Support to Rural Entrepreneurship, Investment and Trade program, and PNG officials met with US officials in Honolulu early this year to talk about a security agreement. At the same time, it has maintained its trade and investment talks with China. It will be difficult for any country to influence PNG to view China in a different way.

PNG has applied the Melanesian approach of a "quick compromise" when in conflict with other states, which has facilitated a smooth working bilateral relationship with many countries. The "bully beef" trade war with Fiji, Australia's opposition to the use of Sandline International mercenaries in the Bougainville crisis, and the short-lived attempt to shift its diplomatic recognition to Taiwan are examples of quick compromises in PNG foreign policy.

Australia must understand that its own economy is huge and it could potentially withstand sanctions imposed by China if engaged in a conflict. However, PNG, with a small manufacturing sector and considerable dependency on the sales of its natural resources to the Chinese market, will struggle greatly if it joins a multinational team or any other anti-China group.

The majority of Chinese retail and wholesale businesses in PNG which source products from China, New Zealand or Australia will also be affected, resulting in inflation. The retail and wholesale sector is dominated by Chinese businesses. Australian retail and wholesale businesses such as Coles, Woolworths and Kmart do not have outlets in PNG.

Those commercial ties mean that a security cooperation agreement between PNG and China for training security personnel and providing vital security resources is necessary. PNG authorities must be able to deal with law-and-order issues in the different towns and cities to help protect the many Chinese retail and wholesale businesses.

Since Marape came to office, PNG's relations with Australia have grown to another level. He could, as Medcalf suggests, work with a multinational team to contain the risk posed by China in the Pacific region. He remains unpredictable and is not afraid to make risky decisions, such as the closure of the Porgera goldmine. But such a move by Marape would be inconsistent with PNG's foreign policy and not in its best interests.

Other lesser powers in the Pacific region might be able to work with an Australia-led multinational team but PNG will not. Australia must respect PNG's position and see how best it can work with PNG as an equal.

Bernard Yegiora is a lecturer in the Department of PNG Studies and International Relations at the Divine Word University.

Nic Maclellan

Rory Medcalf's essay "Sea of Many Flags" brought to mind the famous encounter in *Crocodile Dundee*, where the hero faced a gang of knife-wielding hoodlums. "That's not a knife," Mick Dundee drawls, pulling out his razor-sharp bowie knife. "THAT's a knife."

I agree with Mick Dundee: Medcalf, the head of ANU's National Security College, needs to define his terms if he wants to go knife-fighting in the Indo-Pacific.

In his essay, Medcalf says: "China appears to want a permanent armed foothold in the Pacific." Such euphemisms avoid defining whether we're talking about a wharf and fuel supply or a vast military-industrial complex the size of Pearl Harbor in Hawai'i or Apra Harbor Naval Station in Guam. The idea that China is using infrastructure funding to establish military bases in the Pacific is firmly entrenched in Australian debate. Yet Medcalf, like much media and academic commentary, downplays key realities around logistics, distance, land tenure and cost that constrain construction of a Chinese base.

It's easy to find detailed studies on the difficulties of building military installations in low-lying atoll nations. As one example, the US Army recently funded two detailed RAND Corporation studies on China's Global Basing Ambitions, which ranked Fiji and Papua New Guinea as "medium desirability" but "low feasibility" for Chinese base construction, while Solomon Islands and Kiribati are not feasible: "Although China's pursuit of basing or access in Oceania may raise concerns for the United States and other countries in the Indo-Pacific, only three Pacific Island Countries – PNG, Fiji and Timor Leste – did not score extremely poorly in terms of feasibility."

Medcalf suggests that the Chinese government started the region's current geopolitical contest, arguing that it "was not due to some hawkish Washington plot, but was an imposition from Beijing". I'd suggest, using his own words, "this is false, both as narrative and chronology".

Some of us are old enough to remember the cries of "the Russians are coming" from Australian military strategists, projecting the Pacific as an "American Lake" – the title of an excellent 1986 study that analysed Indo-Pacific dynamics long before the concept was reinvented by the ANU National Security College. As a journalist, I wrote articles about Russian and Chinese forces in the Pacific islands more than a quarter of a century ago. Well before today's China industry discovered the islands, the late Ron Crocombe – a doyen of Pacific studies – wrote *Asia in the Pacific: Replacing the West*. His massive tome analysed China's role alongside that of Korea, Indonesia, Malaysia and other emerging Asian powerhouses.

Of course, it's crucial to monitor and analyse China's ongoing role as a trade, security and diplomatic partner, but it helps to recognise the agency of island governments and communities and know a bit of regional history. Breathless commentary about Kiribati's 2019 switch of diplomatic ties from Taiwan to the PRC rarely mentions that Kiribati backed Beijing over Taipei until 2003. The recent shift back to China is a return to past policy, not an unprecedented PRC diplomatic breakthrough.

Medcalf argues that "most of the published Indo-Pacific policy documents are consistent with other collective Pacific statements" adopted by the Pacific Islands Forum, such as the 2018 Boe Declaration or the 2050 Strategy for the Blue Pacific Continent. I'd argue the opposite. Name one Indo-Pacific strategy from a Western power that puts climate change at the very centre of its security analysis!

Last year, I interviewed President Louis Mapou, the first pro-independence leader of New Caledonia in forty years. The Kanak politician stressed that "the issues of emancipation and self-determination are principles that underly the Forum's 2050 Strategy". Yet most Indo-Pacific analysts ignore or downplay the right to self-determination and decolonisation in US, New Zealand and French territories. They are silent on UN opposition to the deployment of military forces in colonial dependencies. As Mapou told me: "When people talk about possible military bases in countries like Solomon Islands, we wonder – where is the discussion about the military agreements that France has in the region through its territories?"

The absence of indigenous voices from Guam, New Caledonia and French Polynesia in Medcalf's essay isn't surprising. Island leaders are sidelined from many key summits that drive Indo-Pacific policy formulation, from AUKUS to the Quad. A January 2023 inquiry into France's Indo-Pacific Strategy by the French Senate's Foreign Affairs, Defence and National Security Committee had the honesty to admit that Kanak and Ma'ohi politicians "were not consulted by the metropolitan executive power prior to the adoption of the strategy, or, more recently, the deployment of military forces in their territories".

Medcalf wants Australia and its allies to "dilute China's influence" in the region. He modestly acknowledges that "others may have capabilities and ideas more suited for Pacific needs than our own – perhaps Japanese technical expertise, French marine research, German democratic transparency, Indian health care or British climate finance". But his list misses one obvious group – Pacific islanders!

The essay calls for an "'oceans forum' where nations such as Fiji, Papua New Guinea, Solomon Islands and Vanuatu could share notes with, say, Maldives, Mauritius, Seychelles and Sri Lanka on parallel challenges". Surely Medcalf has heard of the Alliance of Small Island States (AOSIS), founded in 1990, that serves this very purpose? Or the Organisation of African Caribbean and Pacific States? Small Island Developing States drove the adoption of Sustainable Development Goal 14 on the oceans and seas, played a crucial role in the recent finalisation of the new high seas treaty and have led UN discussion on the ocean–climate nexus.

This refusal to acknowledge decades of South–South cooperation and to recognise the successes of Oceanic diplomacy highlights everything that's wrong with Australian dreams of leadership in the Indo-Pacific.

Today, "we're listening to Pacific voices" is a bipartisan message from Canberra. The problem, however, is not about listening. For decades, Pacific island governments have repeatedly outlined their objectives for emissions reductions, climate finance and disaster response. Australian politicians have listened and – on occasion – acted. But denial, delay and diversion have dominated Canberra's response, protecting the interests of fossil-fuel corporations.

When it comes to addressing climate change in the Pacific, Western allies have repeatedly failed to deliver. It's little wonder, therefore, that island nations have been willing to engage with new players in the region.

Australia cannot claim a leadership role if it ignores Pacific agency, history and perspectives, and then fails to allocate the staff, finances and institutional support to address the climate crisis – the single greatest threat to the wellbeing and livelihoods of Pacific islanders and to the security of the region itself.

Nic Maclellan is a correspondent for Islands Business *magazine (Fiji) and a contributor to* The China Alternative: Changing Regional Order in the Pacific Islands.

Luke Fletcher

"Sea of Many Flags", Rory Medcalf's expansive and lyrical essay, is framed around two questions: what exactly are China's ambitions in the Southwest Pacific and what should Australia do about them? The essay follows on from his 2020 book, *Contest for the Indo-Pacific*, in which he argued that Australia should team up with a multipolar coalition of nations to counter – or, in his words, to "manage" – growing Chinese power in the region.

Both the book and the essay present an authoritative voice that raises concerns about the rise of China in a way that is balanced, nuanced and reasonable. Medcalf adopts a tone of restraint when talking about China's impact, noting that despite the growth of Chinese aid in the first two decades of the twenty-first century, it still lags behind not only Australia, but also New Zealand and the United States. He is also careful to avoid hyperbole when talking about last year's China–Solomons security pact, unlike many in the Australian media at the time. And the essay calls not for the exclusion of "one of the world's greatest powers from the largest oceans", but for an "inclusive vision for long-term development and protection of sovereignty". Yet Australia and its allies have often fallen short – just as China has – in their attempts to foster inclusive development and a just response to the impacts of climate change in the Pacific.

Medcalf is unsure how to characterise China's strategy in the Pacific. He asks: is it trying to establish a region-wide hegemony to eventually challenge American global primacy? Or are the intricate economic webs China is spinning across the region the lattice over which military and political elements of control will be built? Whatever the intention, as Medcalf concludes, the outcome will be the Chinese establishment of "wealth, control and presence" in the region. He believes this is an outcome which Australia should oppose, arguing that can be done by a combination of drawing on Australia's allies in the region (New Zealand, the US, Japan, France and India, to name a few) and a "quieter" kind of Pacific leadership, characterised by "self-awareness, inclusion and genuine diplomacy".

Ultimately, whether one agrees with Medcalf's exposition of the problem will have as much to do with how one understands the actions of Australia as by one's views on China. Recent publications by David Brophy (*China Panic*) and Clinton Fernandes (*Sub-Imperial Power*) characterise Australia's actions in the Pacific as being driven primarily by a desire to exert hegemony over the Pacific to maintain it as a stable part of the US world-system (or, in the parlance of diplomacy, the "rules-based international order").

While I agree with this view, it does not follow that Medcalf is fundamentally wrong in his depiction of Chinese behaviour. China is seeking to extend its economic reach into the Pacific's natural resources, as it is in other parts of the world, to solidify its place at the centre of the world's key supply chains for agriculture, timber, fisheries and minerals. It *has* secured lucrative business contracts and consultancies in the region. It *has* tried to secure potential military bases in the Pacific, as the 2022 agreement with Solomon Islands attests, and is seeking more. And its aid and other diplomatic offerings will likely help it to secure more resources, contracts and military agreements.

But no one is innocent here. The reality is that Malaysian companies dominate illegal logging, Chinese firms do much of the overfishing and Australian, Canadian and American mining companies have led the way in mineral and petroleum extraction. Together, all these nations and more have conspired to strip the region of its resources. It is true that China has placed itself at the midpoint of many of the supply chains by receiving and processing almost all of the raw timber and much of the minerals and seafood products. But the exploitation of the Pacific is a global team effort.

In the meantime, Australia talks about opening new coalmines and gasfields and investing tens of billions in defence against China (including in the Pacific), yet only gives pennies towards climate adaptation or loss and damage financing, and creates a problematic infrastructure loan facility for the Pacific which perverts our aid program. This, even as storms and cyclones lash the region and Pacific communities see their water resources turn brackish and their burial grounds inundated by the sea. If we are going to talk about "self-awareness" to counter Chinese influence in the Pacific region, then looking at the development model Australia is helping to facilitate, and adopting real (as opposed to pretend) climate policies might be a good place to start.

Luke Fletcher is the executive director of the Jubilee Australia Research Centre and a visiting fellow at the UNSW School of Social Sciences.

Rory Medcalf responds

The point of Australian Foreign Affairs is to drive debate. It looks like my essay about a multipolar response to China's Pacific powerplay has done its bit in that regard, as attested by the four substantial responses it has prompted, from Zhou Fangyin, Bernard Yegiora, Nic Maclellan and Luke Fletcher. I thank them for their trouble, and for the thoughtful (and, in Maclellan's case, cinematically entertaining) approach they've taken.

Despite the rather dramatic title of the issue, *Girt by China*, and the recent context of security anxiety in the Australian policy debate, my thesis is not that China should somehow be shut out of the Pacific or that Australian defence imperatives should override the interests of our Pacific neighbours.

Instead, I sought to write something that could help reconcile Australian strategic concerns with the vital human and environmental security interests of Pacific communities. There's a virtuous circle between diluting China's bid for regional dominance and providing a range of development and security partners to smaller countries. This parallels the implicit purpose of Canberra's current statecraft.

Luke Fletcher acknowledges my balanced approach. In the correspondence from Nic Maclellan and Zhou Fangyin, on the other hand, one senses some frustration that the essay has not presented a larger or less ambiguous target. Indeed, Zhou tries to simplify things by claiming that I accuse China of "attempting to dominate the Pacific region as part of its challenge to the United States globally". In fact, my piece very specifically defines such an attempt at dominance as just one of multiple possible futures, noting that the speed and scale of China's influence brings risk even if there is no such strategic agenda. Accidental empires can still bring strife.

The essay was not meant to be an all-encompassing treatment of wrongs inflicted on the region, from indigenous dispossession to corporate greed and climate complacency. Fletcher is quite right: no power is innocent here. My piece was no apologia for empires past; instead, it warns that China runs the risk of following in colonial footsteps with destabilising speed. Nor was it framed as patronising guidance for the governments or communities of Pacific island states about how best to advance and protect their interests. That is their business.

Rather, a purpose of "Sea of Many Flags" was to highlight how multipolarity can work to the advantage of regional countries by providing a wealth of options for partners in development, sustainability, prosperity, security and governance. From an Australian policy perspective, this means that we should not try to be everything to all Pacific countries, and we should get better at identifying and helping to coordinate the value and goodwill that others bring.

In this, I am guilty of advocating a kind of Australian leadership in the Pacific. This is informed by an assumption that perhaps should have been stated plainly near the start of the essay. Australia's strategic interests and relative weight in the Pacific mean that we can expect this country to pursue leadership of one sort or another, no matter what. Best, therefore, that it be quiet and Pacific in character, marked by self-awareness and inclusion, not a geopolitics-centric indifference to Pacific perspectives or needs.

Maclellan misreads my essay as somehow excluding Pacific island states as capable partners in their own development. If that was what the essay said, then I'd gladly join him in criticising it. Instead, I noted at the outset that any conversation on the international relations of the Pacific should be grounded in the interests, values and identity of Pacific nations, while part of its conclusion recommended that Australia should work to ensure that Pacific voices are at the table at every stage. Australia should be willing to sometimes step back. True, I don't then provide detailed sections explaining precisely how all Pacific nations can be partners to one another, because the article was about providers of development and security from beyond the immediate Pacific neighbourhood. In retrospect, excluding the paragraph on New Zealand would have made this point clearer – but it was there partly to counter false and predictable claims that Australia's alignments in the Pacific are all about serving America.

While I respect Fletcher and Maclellan as Australians deeply engaged in the challenges facing Pacific communities, and welcome Zhou's confidence that China will not pressure Pacific governments, there is particular value in Yegiora's correspondence. Here is a genuinely Pacific voice providing a firm sense of the national interests of a key Pacific nation: Papua New Guinea.

Interestingly, Yegiora's thesis is not that Australia should abjure a leadership role, but rather that PNG should stay out of any multinational coalition to counter China's influence. This is reinforced with arguments that PNG needs China as a development partner and would suffer harm if it displeased Beijing. Both those supporting arguments are compelling. They provide further reasons to encourage a diversification of democratic friends from near and far, and the strengthening of frameworks for regional solidarity.

Finally, where I agree with all four correspondents is on the need for Australia to honour the standards it promotes: on security, environmental stewardship, governance, transparency and rules. Whatever the misdeeds or missteps of the past, this will be essential to Australia's credibility now and in the future – however China's presence unfolds.

Rory Medcalf is a professor and head of the National Security College at the Australian National University.

Subscribe to Australian Foreign Affairs & save up to 28% on the cover price.

Enjoy free home delivery of the print edition and full digital as well as ebook access to the journal via the Australian Foreign Affairs website and app for Android and iPhone users.

Forthcoming issue:
The New Domino Theory
(October 2023)

Never miss an issue. Subscribe and save.

☐ **1 year auto-renewing print and digital subscription** (3 issues) $49.99 within Australia. Outside Australia $79.99*.

☐ **1 year print and digital subscription** (3 issues) $59.99 within Australia. Outside Australia $99.99.

☐ **1 year auto-renewing digital subscription** (3 issues) $29.99.*

☐ **2 year print and digital subscription** (6 issues) $114.99 within Australia.

☐ **1 year auto-renewing digital Quarterly Essay and Australian Foreign Affairs bundle subscription** (7 issues) $69.99.*

☐ Tick here to commence subscription with the current issue.

Give an inspired gift. Subscribe a friend.

☐ **1 year print and digital gift subscription** (3 issues) $59.99 within Australia. Outside Australia $99.99.

☐ **1 year digital-only gift subscription** (3 issues) $29.99.

☐ **2 year print and digital gift subscription** (6 issues) $114.99 within Australia.

☐ **1 year digital-only Quarterly Essay and Australian Foreign Affairs bundle gift subscription** (7 issues) $69.99.

☐ Tick here to commence subscription with the current issue.

ALL PRICES INCLUDE GST, POSTAGE AND HANDLING.

*Your subscription will automatically renew until you notify us to stop. Prior to the end of your subscription period, we will send you a reminder notice.

Please turn over for subscription order form, or subscribe online at **australianforeignaffairs.com**
Alternatively, call 1800 077 514 or +61 3 9486 0288 or email **subscribe@australianforeignaffairs.com**

Back Issues

ALL PRICES INCLUDE GST, POSTAGE AND HANDLING.

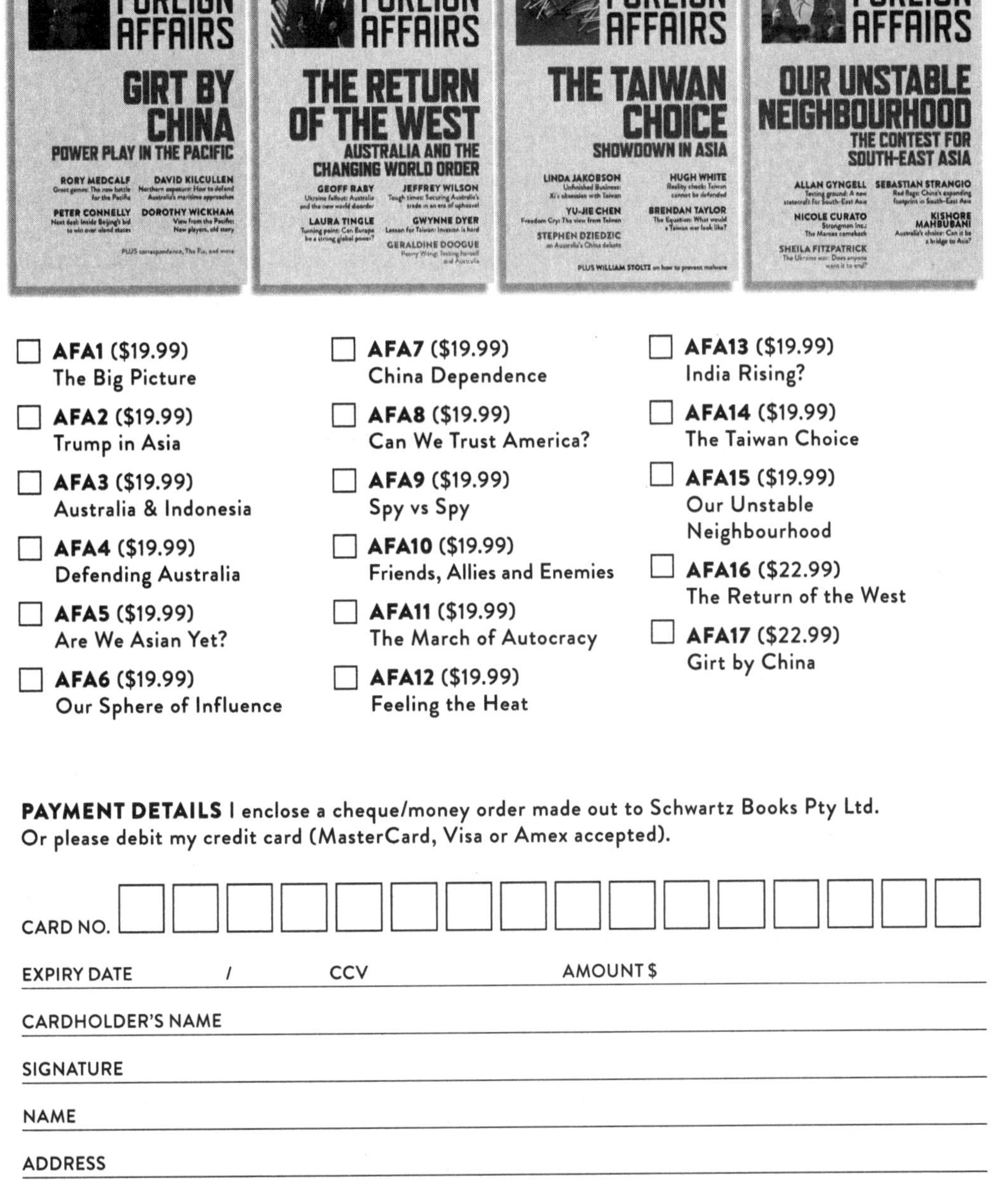

- ☐ **AFA1** ($19.99) The Big Picture
- ☐ **AFA2** ($19.99) Trump in Asia
- ☐ **AFA3** ($19.99) Australia & Indonesia
- ☐ **AFA4** ($19.99) Defending Australia
- ☐ **AFA5** ($19.99) Are We Asian Yet?
- ☐ **AFA6** ($19.99) Our Sphere of Influence
- ☐ **AFA7** ($19.99) China Dependence
- ☐ **AFA8** ($19.99) Can We Trust America?
- ☐ **AFA9** ($19.99) Spy vs Spy
- ☐ **AFA10** ($19.99) Friends, Allies and Enemies
- ☐ **AFA11** ($19.99) The March of Autocracy
- ☐ **AFA12** ($19.99) Feeling the Heat
- ☐ **AFA13** ($19.99) India Rising?
- ☐ **AFA14** ($19.99) The Taiwan Choice
- ☐ **AFA15** ($19.99) Our Unstable Neighbourhood
- ☐ **AFA16** ($22.99) The Return of the West
- ☐ **AFA17** ($22.99) Girt by China

PAYMENT DETAILS I enclose a cheque/money order made out to Schwartz Books Pty Ltd.
Or please debit my credit card (MasterCard, Visa or Amex accepted).

CARD NO. ☐☐☐☐☐☐☐☐☐☐☐☐☐☐☐☐

EXPIRY DATE   /   CCV   AMOUNT $

CARDHOLDER'S NAME

SIGNATURE

NAME

ADDRESS

EMAIL   PHONE

Post or fax this form to: Reply Paid 90094, Collingwood VIC 3066 **Freecall:** 1800 077 514 **or** +61 3 9486 0288
Fax: (03) 9011 6106 **Email:** subscribe@australianforeignaffairs.com **Website:** australianforeignaffairs.com
Subscribe online at australianforeignaffairs.com/subscribe (please do not send electronic scans of this form)

The Back Page

FOREIGN POLICY CONCEPTS AND JARGON, EXPLAINED

POLYCRISIS

What is it: The simultaneous occurrence of multiple global catastrophes. The Cascade Institute (research centre, Canada) says a polycrisis must include at least three events. It is different from a "permacrisis", which can involve lurching from one crisis to another.

Who coined it: The term was first used in the late 1990s by Edgar Morin (theorist, French National Centre for Scientific Research), who believed explanations for global and ecological challenges are often wrongly reduced to single causes.

Who revived it? In 2016, Jean-Claude Juncker (former president, European Commission) popularised the term when he claimed the European Union had emerged from a polycrisis involving a debt crisis, a migrant crisis, Brexit and rising populism. In 2022, Adam Tooze (historian, Columbia University) began using the term to describe the shocks caused by the COVID-19 pandemic, climate change, China–US tensions and the war in Ukraine.

Who likes it? Tooze insists standard crises can be attributed to single causes, such as market forces, but a polycrisis is "like a bad breakfast buffet ... it's an indigestible mixture of ingredients that do not normally go together". Lawrence Summers (former Treasury secretary, US) agrees, saying he "cannot remember ... as many cross-currents as there are right now".

Who doesn't? Others say the term is useless and the world is always in a polycrisis. Gideon Rachman (commentator, *Financial Times*) described it as "one of my least favourite cliches". Niall Ferguson (fellow, Hoover Institution), during a panel with Tooze at the World Economic Forum in Davos in January 2023, said: "It's just history happening."